OWNER'S GUIDE TO

Better Behavior

IN DOGS & CATS

OWNER'S GUIDE TO

Better Behavior

IN DOGS & CATS

By

William E. Campbell

Illustrated by Robert M. Miller, DVM

Alpine Publications Inc.

2456 E. 9th St. • Loveland, CO 80537

ISBN No. 0-931866-42-1

Printed in the United States of America.

Cover photo: William B. Dewey
Cover design: Russell Shultz

Most Alpine Books are available at special quantity discounts for bulk purchases for club promotions, premiums, fund raising, breeder "litter lots", or educational use. Special books or book excerpts can also be created to fit specific needs.

For details, write or telephone Special Markets, Alpine Publications, 214 19th St. S.E., Loveland, CO 80537; (303) 667-2017.

Table of Contents

Introduction

Several years ago I wrote *Behavior Problems in Dogs* as a textbook for students of pet-dog behavior, especially veterinarians. It is still popular and useful, but too technical as a "How-To" guide for the average pet owner.

This second book uses the language I use with my own clients, avoiding the jargon of animal behaviorists, so you can select and raise a puppy or kitten or solve a behavior problem without feeling you are cramming for a college degree.

I am delighted that the inimitable RMM (Robert M. Miller, DVM) agreed to illustrate many of the ideas. As an outstanding veterinarian and a talented cartoonist, Bob conveys insight and cheerful optimism about even the grimmest situations. I know you will get more than a few chuckles along the way to solving your problems.

This is a "How-To" book, but it also explains *why* you should do certain things. For instance, you'll find several references to a correction procedure called the "Jolly Routine." If you did not understand *why* I ask you to clap hands, jump up and merrily run about bouncing a ball as a step in rehabilitating an aggressive dog, I doubt that you'd be motivated to do so.

However, when you discover the role of the dog's orienting reflex, and how a pet interprets its owner's actions and emotions, then you are on the way to a solution that ends with the dog greeting guests with a wagging tail and an invitation to play, instead of acting like a four-footed meat grinder.

I entered this field almost 20 years ago, convinced that pet owners did not *want* to inflict physical or psychologic pain on their canine and feline family members. I am even more sure of it today. I know you will be pleased to find that various punishments, and even scolding, are not part of my correction program. Punishment hurts more than your pet; it harms your relationship with it. As you will see, a positive relationship is the foundation for teaching a pet to feel and behave differently.

Techniques to Avoid

Speaking of punishment, I will mention some of the supposedly more "refined" techniques being bandied about lately, that you will *not* find here. This may prevent you from mixing those methods with mine, which could be even worse than doing nothing at all.

7

Electrical Shock Devices

Even with fancy labels such as "Hi-Tech" and "electrical stimulation," shocking a pet dog to control unwanted behavior is a quick-fix method that is totally out of step with enlightened, humane approaches.

Cages

I have never found caging necessary. In my experience, most people who recommend cages also sell or rent them. I receive calls every week from owners with caged dogs, for help in housetraining, self-mutilation, unruliness and aggressive problems, all stemming from the "zoo-dog syndrome." I also never recommend putting a dog outdoors, in garages, bedrooms or closets as a means of "psychological" punishment for misbehavior.

Rough Handling

I have met too many dog trainers with scarred hands, arms or faces to recommend any rough handling of a dog or puppy to gain physical dominance or correct behavior problems. Shaking or roughly pressing a dog into submission is not necessary to gain leadership, and risks creating unwanted side effects, such as submissive wetting, or biting. Besides, 90-pound owners with 125-pound dogs have difficulty with the technique!

Among other physical measures not to be found here are "kneeing" your dog in the chest, stepping on its toes or throwing it on its back to stop jumping; submerging the dog's head in a water-filled, freshly dug hole, until the animal goes limp, to correct digging.

With any of these heavy-handed measures there is a greater chance of damaging your relationship with your pet than of solving problem behavior.

Food Rewards

Giving a dog food treats in order to change behavior is another method getting a lot of "ink" from experts with backgrounds in *experimental* animal behavior, rather than experience with real-life pet owners and their animals. Food rewards are potent motivators, but by themselves they fail to address the *causes* of unwanted behavior.

If you get the idea that I place a lot of faith in the dog's ability to live in a human family as a dependable, well-behaved, loyal companion, without needing to be shocked, shaken, wrestled, shouted or stared at, bribed or beaten into submission, then I have made my first important point. The second point is to prove it! That is what the rest of this book is about.

William E. Campbell
Grants Pass, Oregon

Acknowledgments

This book is the result of the influences of countless people on my life. It would be impossible to list all of them. However, I want to mention those who provided "turning points" and motivated me to work to develop better ways of solving problems. I acknowledge with deep gratitude:

- *the man who showed me that authority is not always wise nor correct: my Dad,* **Edward A. Campbell**
- *the woman who guided me to read, long before school age: my Mom,* **Lillian E. Campbell**
- *the master of management training who helped me to recognize the difference between objectives and problems:* **Louis A. Backer**
- *the management consultant who helped me realize that true motivation comes from within and responds to leadership, rather than manipulation, promises or threats:* **David Warren Piper**
- *the ethologist who demonstrated that pet dogs learn best from their owners, and who pioneered the "causative" approach to dog behavior problems:* **Dare Miller**
- *the veterinarian and past editor of* Modern Veterinary Practice *whose labors on this manuscript and others since 1972 have crystallized so many new ideas:* **J. Frederick Smithcors**
- *the veterinarian whose invitation to lecture at his UCLA extension programs made me formalize my approach to behavior problems:* **Herbert N. Snow**
- *the veterinarian and teacher whose vision led to the formation of the American Society of Veterinary Ethology in 1975:* **Bonnie Beaver**
- *the author and sage who revealed the path toward an ideal: to be in the world, but not of it; to be free from ambition, greed, intellectual pride, blind obedience to custom, or awe of those higher in rank; to understand that an attitude, like a virtue or a vice, cannot be taught, it must be "caught":* **Idries Shah**

- *that marvelous Dalmatian who confirmed my belief that dogs thrive when they can function as part of a family, as she sniffed out and fetched the daily newspaper, tail wagging, waiting for a "Good dog" and a gentle pat, even though she was totally blind; bless you,* **"Tally"**
- *all those who continually prove that sensible, humane correction programs really do succeed: the thousands of veterinarians who regularly dispense the BehavioR$_x$ Client Education programs to millions of dog and cat owners*
- *the editor who brought together the words and the pictures and made this a book:* **Roxanne Lapidus**

- *the lady whose contributions are on every page, yet defy any verbal description: my wife,* **Peggy**

Foreword

The symbiotic relationship between man and dog goes back to the earliest phases of mankind's development. Both creatures were hunters. Both lived in small groups—a band or pack—and both were governed by a complex social order. Both species lived by their wits, lacking the physical power of the great predators, such as the lion and the sabre-toothed tiger, and used strategy and the strength of numbers to bring home game.

The puppy fit into the primitive cave domicile, serving as a playmate for human children, an entertaining companion for the adults, and was the source and recipient of affection and stroking. The dog's keener senses were invaluable to man in guarding his territory, and in locating, pursuing and bringing down game.

Much later, when man became a pastoral nomad, the dog herded his flocks. The fact that man often abused the dog, and sometimes ate him, doesn't alter the intensely close relationship between the two species.

Thus, man and dog have an extremely long and traditional relationship. Most persons instinctively like dogs. Watch a toddler as a friendly dog approaches. Observe people of all ages as they crowd up to the pet shop window. The dog is historically secure in his place as man's best friend.

The sciences of human psychology and human behavior are a mere century old. The sciences of animal behavior and ethology (comparative behavior) are much younger. We are only beginning to understand that each species inherits behavioral characteristics peculiar to it, which helped that species to survive and develop in a hostile world.

There are many differences between the inherent behavioral characteristics of man and dog. Our imprinting and learning patterns differ. We signal aggression, submission, territorial possession, the desire to play, and the desire to mate in very different ways. Yet, as we shall see in Bill Campbell's excellent and perceptive book, there are many similarities between our behavior and that of our canine friends.

11

Campbell's techniques go beyond the usual dog trainer's rote and often fallacious methods. He examines, understands and uses the dog's inherent responses to produce a well-adjusted dog. One of life's greatest pleasures, indeed, is a mannerly and well-adjusted dog. Most of us know that and crave such a relationship. Too often, however, things don't go as we had hoped, and we end up with a misbehaving dog. A dog that misbehaves is no joy. In fact, it can be a great problem, a stress, a liability, and even a danger.

Bill's book brings to the average literate dog owner an *understanding* of basic canine behavior, together with *techniques* to produce a well-mannered and happy dog.

R.M. Miller, DVM
Thousand Oaks, California

1
Understanding
Behavior Problems

or

Problem, Problem, Who's Got the Problem?

Dogs don't often suffer from behavior problems; people do. In fact, dogs as a general rule don't even *cause* behavior problems. We owners are the culprits. Further, most so-called dog behavior problems don't rate any serious attention until they make people uncomfortable enough to do something about them. Then, all too often, a solution to the problem appears logically to be "fix the dog." That is, when the dog starts the unwanted behavior, do something to stop it and/or make the animal do something else. This is the *behavioral* approach. The trouble with this system is that it deals with symptoms, not causes, as we will see.

Another, more enlightened view is to deduce that the dog behavior leading to the human discomfort is not the problem in itself, but is a *symptom* of some internal condition the pet suffers from, popularly called *anxiety*. The difficulty with this method is that it tries to do something to the anxiety. It usually ignores the reasons for the anxiety.

A third approach views the dog as more than a simple "behavioral model" that responds to various stimuli by behaving in wanted or unwanted ways. This method recognizes a pet dog (or cat) as a four-legged member of a two-legged family, with most of the emotional attachments and involvements shared by its human companions. This approach sees the unwanted behavior as a way for the dog to relieve the tension created by anxiety, which is caused by some sort of frustration in the pet's life. For want of a more descriptive name, I call this a *causative* approach to behavior problems.

13

To get a clear picture of how these three approaches work, let's take a classic case history from my files and analyze it. I'll present it as if you are the dog's owner. Case histories are more fun when you imagine the problem is personal. This problem is one of the most difficult to correct: barking when left home alone.

THE CASE OF THE BARKING DOG

Your pet is a good-natured, medium-sized spayed terrier-mix, two years old. You live in an adults-only apartment building and have had the same neighbors since your dog was a puppy. Until recently you and all your neighbors worked the usual five-day week, but then the man next door went on a midnight to 8:00 AM shift.

You knew your dog always barked when you went to work, but nobody complained, so it wasn't a problem. In fact, you felt lucky, because one neighbor had a dog that chewed up carpets when it was left alone. At least barking wasn't destructive.

Last night, however, your perspective changed. The landlord knocked on your door and presented a legal barking-dog complaint from the city's animal regulation department, and an eviction warning.

Now who has a problem? Several parties, in fact! The neighbor who signed the complaint feels badly about it, but he has to sleep in order to keep working. The landlord dislikes evicting anyone but has to live by the rules, so he gives you the legal month to get the situation solved, apologizes, and starts mentally preparing a want ad for your apartment. And you. Do you have problems! All sorts of things are going around in your head.

You feel like calling the neighbor and saying, "Thanks, Ralph! The least you could've done was to have spoken to me about it before you sicced the law on me! And by the way, forget about that patio barbeque next Saturday night!" But you decide to pull your emotional harness tight and investigate ways to solve the problem and remain in your happy home.

What to Do?

Let's look at your alternatives in a framework of possible solutions and usual results. First, those from most popular books and behaviorists.

Problem = Barking Dog

Solution   **Usual outcome**

 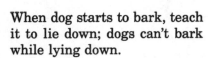 

When dog starts to bark, teach it to lie down; dogs can't bark while lying down.

Not so. Dog either learns to bark while prone, or waits until you're gone to bark.

  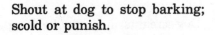

Shout at dog to stop barking; scold or punish.

Dog stops barking when you shout, scold or punish. Waits until you've gone to start again.

Problem = Barking Dog
(continued)

Solution   **Usual Outcome**

Muzzle the dog.   Muffled barking, thirsty dog.

Strap on an electric shock collar; "zap" dog when it barks.

May stop barking when collar is on, but heightens anxiety and dog may substitute other behavior, such as chewing furniture, self.

Surgically remove dog's vocal cords.

Dog screams, may start barking again if cords grow back.

Problem = Barking Dog
(continued)

Treat anxiety by getting dog to sit quietly before you leave it, instead of acting anxious, excitable. Give it a delicious tidbit as reward.

Fat, barking dog.

Treat anxiety by giving dog tranquilizer, sleeping pill, or other medication.

Calm, or sleepy, barking dog, Sometimes stops barking, but drugs have long-term adverse side-effects. Barking recurs when drug withdrawn.

There are variations to these approaches, but the theme remains the same; treat the barking behavior and/or anxiety. I do not mean to indicate that these treatments do not work to stop barking in some cases. They must, because a lot of books and fairly high-priced animal behaviorists are peddling them, often in combination with elaborate ways for you to become dominant over your dog by acting like a dog yourself. We'll discuss this aspect later. For now, let's consider an approach to your barking dog problem that reaches beyond behavior and anxiety, and looks at what is going on in your day-to-day life with the terrier.

The Causative Approach

What is causing the frustration that creates the anxiety and tension the dog is attempting to relieve by the barking? When you uncover the answer to this question, and do something about it, the barking can stop in an amazingly short time—a couple of days in some cases, as long as six weeks in others. However, there's a catch. You are the only person who knows what's bugging your dog, and only you can take the steps necessary to correct the situation and make the threat of eviction go away. So, let's pretend you find a specialist in dog behavior problems who uses the *causative* approach. At the appointed time, the doorbell rings. (This person makes house calls, though many do not.)

The Fact-finding Routine

For the moment we'll ignore exactly what is being said in your conversation and describe what is happening, as if you two are Greek and I don't speak the language, except that I recognize your names, the dog's name (Tippy), and the Greek for "Come," "Sit" and "No." This is about the limit of Tippy's knowledge of spoken words as well.

The Scene

As the doorbell rings, the dog runs to the door ahead of you. You open the door, trying to get your leg between Tippy and the specialist, George.

George and you exchange greetings while Tippy is jumping up and yipping at both. George reaches to pet Tippy, who rolls onto her side. George pets her briefly. You close the door and gesture toward the living room. The dog runs ahead and jumps and yips at George while he sits. You sit on a chair opposite George and call Tippy to you. She

ignores you. You stand and start toward George and Tippy, calling the dog. Tippy rolls onto her side again. You pick her up, return to the chair and put her down into a sitting position at your feet. The conversation continues while Tippy whines. You say "No" to her, shaking her by the scruff of neck. You get up to go to the kitchen to turn on the coffee maker. Tippy races after you. George gets out his notepad, and makes notes.

Tippy returns to the room, followed by you. You call Tippy to the chair, tell her to sit, and stroke her. She stays calm as long as you keep stroking, while the conversation continues. When you stop stroking, Tippy whines, and gets restless. You stroke again. You get up to go to the kitchen for coffee and cups. There is the same routine, with Tippy following you out, leading you back.

For the first half-hour George asks questions, and you do most of the talking. Then, George takes over, evidently explaining his recommendations, since he is writing on a form and showing it to you occasionally.

(Now I must refer to what George is saying, so what follows makes sense.) He says he is going to have you learn by using the power of nonverbal communication with Tippy. He explains that, without speaking a word to the dog, you are about to teach Tippy to stay by your chair, without any anxiety or excitement, while you go to the door to say goodbye to him. *Fat chance,* you think.

George starts to stir, as if to get ready to leave, and you start to get up. Tippy starts wagging her tail, and jumping again at George, who is sidling toward the door. You go toward the door and Tippy runs ahead. Both you and George return to your seats. Tippy leaves the door, tentatively, and returns to you, wagging her tail. You pet her briefly (two seconds).

You get up, and start to the door. Tippy rushes ahead; you return to your seat. Tippy returns to you and you pet her briefly. You again get up, and start to the door. Tippy sits at your chair, looking expectantly at you. You return to the chair and pet Tippy briefly. This get-up/go-to-door/return-pet routine goes on for 15 minutes, until you finally can open and close the door while Tippy remains at the chair.

George then accompanies you to the door, at which time Tippy leaves the chair and races ahead. You both return to your chairs; so does Tippy. You pet her briefly. However, only five minutes' worth of the going/returning is required before Tippy remains at your chair while the door is opened for George to leave, after which you return to your chair, a thoughtful expression on your face, and George's recommendation sheet in your hand.

As you sit down you absent-mindedly reach down to pet Tippy, but suddenly withdraw your hand, looking rather sheepishly at your instructions.

What George Learned

Before revealing what was said during the interview, let's peek at George's private notepad to see what he wrote when you went to get the coffee.

George's First Notes:
1. Tippy excitable, vocal, good-natured, bossy.
2. Tippy feels leader. Too dependent.
3. Owner too physically dominant-negative vocal.
4. Wrong, too-long pet.

If we review the scenario, it becomes more clear where George got his diagnosis during the first part of the interview. Tippy's center-of-attention behavior during the greeting, her yips and jumping resulted in note #1.

Tippy's leading into the living room, out of the kitchen, back to the door, and following you to the kitchen formed observation #2.

Tippy's extremely submissive response to George's reaching to pet, your own approach when she did not leave George's chair, your loud "No" and scruff-shaking created comment #3.

Your continual stroking to keep Tippy calm accounted for #4.

Now, on to what was said.

The Dialogue

Rather than quote the actual conversation, which space does not allow, let's see what came out about your life with Tippy that is causing the frustration, then see what George suggests you do.

Most of the early part of the interview you spent telling George about your workday and weekend routines. He also wanted to know about early housetraining and behavior problems, especially how you handled them. You tended to tell him what the dog did, to which he responded, "Then what did you do?" or, "How did you react to that?" Here is a list of important practices and events, with recommended changes:

Present Routines	Recommended Changes
You feed Tippy once a day, usually right after coming home in the early evening.	This leaves Tippy with an empty stomach most of the day. Split food, feed AM and PM, with evening meal at least 30 minutes after the latest homecoming time. This avoids "hunger tension" during the day.
You jog with Tippy on weekend mornings, but never during the week.	Jog daily or leave Tippy at home on weekend jogs. Either way provides the consistency Tippy needs.
Before leaving for work, you pick up and cuddle Tippy, reassuring her you'll be back. You put her down away from the door, say "Stay," then hurry out.	This ritual of guilt helps to impress Tippy emotionally that "something is wrong," which she cannot understand, creating frustration. Sit quietly for at least 5 minutes before leaving her. Use walk-to-door/return routine without speaking, in place of "Stay," then leave without speaking.

At homecoming you and Tippy have a joyous greeting ritual at the door.

This builds too much apprehension during the day for Tippy's excitable nature to tolerate. Walk in, say "Hi, Tippy," then do normal homecoming things yourself for 5 minutes. Then greet Tippy away from the front door area.

Whenever Tippy nudges you for affection, you stroke her until she leaves or stops nudging. Whenever you get the urge to give her affection, you go to her and pet and cuddle her.

This "Tippy nudges/you respond" routine helps her feel she is the leader in your relationship. She is never expected to do anything to earn praise and petting. Prolonged stroking helps create an overdependence on your presence, and is too great a contrast to when you are gone. Do *not* withhold affection or petting, but ask Tippy to Come, or Sit when you get the urge or she asks for affection. Then pet her, briefly (less than five seconds), and avoid prolonged stroking. Speak your commands softly, pleasantly.

You taught Tippy to "speak" for tidbits, but rarely do it except when company is present.

Do not tidbit Tippy.

Case Outcome

Improvement was seen during the first week and all unreasonable barking was gone by the middle of the second week. Two further complaints by the neighbor were due to Tippy's barking when salespersons rang the doorbell, which the law allows. On George's advice you got a "Daysleeper—Do Not Disturb" sign for your door.

By the way, you did enjoy that barbeque with your neighbor, after all!

There are further causes, and additional steps are often necessary to correct barking problems, as we will see later. However, this case provides insight about the *causative* approach to behavior problems. Understanding why this approach is so effective requires a closer look at both canine and human nature.

2
The Sensitive Dog

or

*How Dogs See, Smell, Hear, Taste
and Otherwise Sense the World*

We don't have to go into detailed scientific studies of the dog's various senses to understand and solve behavior problems. If you are interested in these, consult the reference reading list. However, it is important to appreciate some of the differences between canine and human perception of our common world. With these in mind, a whole range of problems can be avoided or solved.

SIGHT

Canine eyesight is poor compared to ours when it comes to color perception, or identifying shapes or details within a form (such as noses on faces). But dogs still see things when we are blinded by darkness, and they can perceive something move minutely when we'd bet the family jewels it was motionless. Their wide-angle vision is double ours, while their focus-field is narrower.

If you remember that nature equipped our pets to survive as predators, these variations make sense. A slight movement of a single blade of grass at gathering dusk is detected by the peripheral vision, causing eyes and head to turn almost to the exact spot where the field mouse moved. So begins the stalk for dinner.

This sensitivity to subtle movement helps explain how our pets often seem to know when we are about to get up to leave the house, get dinner ready or go to bed. People unconsciously make minute move-

Canine eyesight is poor compared to ours, in some respects.

ments before taking deliberate actions. Our dogs are astute people-watchers, and use their visual talents to keep up with or, at times, ahead of us.

On the minus side, poor shape, form and detail vision may cause some dogs to become uneasy and others to freak out when they see their owners for the first time doing such things as wearing a hat, using crutches, carrying a pole, or approaching in semidarkness. This is why it's excellent protective policy to speak in an upbeat tone of voice to your dog, or a strange one, in these circumstances.

If you have a dog with hair that hangs over its eyes, do your pet a favor and tie it up or, better yet, cut it off. Life down on the floor is tough enough without having to look at the world through a picket fence. This will avoid visual surprises when people reach to pet or pick up the dog. Contrary to a popular myth, "hairy-eyed" dogs do not go blind when their eyes are exposed to sunlight.

"Did your wife come home with a new hat?"

Later, we'll look into some fascinating, helpful and troublesome reflexes tied to vision.

SMELL

You and I (unless one of us changes form and howls during the full moon) can't even imagine possessing an odor-sensor that can detect a human body buried under a snow avalanche for days, or identify a chemical diluted in a million parts of water. This exquisite sense makes an cvening walk a veritable mental feast for our pets, not just physical exercise.

Noses create problems, too, because dogs have a strong drive to investigate odors, especially if airborne. Many runaway problems start with these.

Our pets use this olfactory sense to identify us and other people and animals. We all exude airborne chemicals from every pore and opening in our bodies. The ones that beget specific responses from kindred animals are called pheromones. For example, a female dog about to come into heat emits messages that can attract male dogs from miles around.

When around people, most pet dogs are content to sniff at a respectable distance for identity odors. However, if they move in close to a

"He probably smells your dog on you."

crotch for more detail, or jump up to gain access to life's very essence, our breath, they violate our human values and find themselves in big trouble. Most such offenders, if caught early enough in their careers, can be corrected if enough people will crouch down to greet them. After a few meetings with several people the dogs are usually content to settle for less intimate introductions.

HEARING

Another dog sense that dwarfs its human counterpart is hearing. Footsteps so soft that a sharp-eared person can't detect them six paces away are heard by dogs when the walker is four times that distance down the street. We really shouldn't be too surprised when our pet starts getting excited before the family car rolls into the driveway or if the barking begins long before the doorbell rings. Most dogs also seem able to select among all sorts of sounds and detect those that are important to them. You'll see this when your dog alerts toward something outdoors with the TV blaring away in the same room. High frequencies, at least double those we can hear, are picked up easily by dogs.

So, if you want to train a dependable watchdog, don't shush it when it barks at what you cannot hear. Instead, help it investigate by cautiously leading it toward the source of the sound. If it is some normal neighborhood sound, such as kids on skateboards, act nonchalant and show the dog there is nothing to get excited about.

When unusual sounds occur (for example, have a friend softly jimmy at a door or window), lead the dog to the scene and get excited yourself. This will help it learn the difference between OK and not-OK noises, thus avoiding the racket of a dog that vocalizes at anything.

Even with this hearing sensitivity, dogs are not particularly talented at discriminating different qualities or characteristics of sounds, especially those of human language. This can lead to many problems between people and their pets. Thus there are folks who believe, "He understands every word I say, but he's just being stubborn!"

Hi-fi Hearing

Dogs have hearing nerves that connect with brain centers functionally akin to human sound centers, but unlike persons, they do not develop anything like our language and speech centers. This is possibly because their voice boxes do not function like ours, and their tongues, lips and mouths are not shaped properly for the kind of speech we develop.

One way to appreciate the dog's perception of our spoken language is to join a foreign language class that uses the conversational approach, rather than the reading method, and forbids students to use English in the classroom. A lot of pointing, touching, moving about, posturing and facial expressions will be used before you learn to do the right things when the teacher looks at you and says: "Venay! Ah-say-yay-voo! Res-tay!"

When you finally do get it, you know that when the teacher makes those sounds you're supposed to "Come, Sit, and Stay," in that order. You also appreciate how important the teacher's expressions of approval are, especially when you start to take the first step toward her in response to the sound "Venay." The expressions of approval (praise) let you know you are thinking about the right thing and motivate you to continue toward the teacher with enthusiasm.

With such positive, socially rewarding systems, people learn basic commands in French almost as quickly as they are learned by dogs! The dog's advantage is its extreme sensitivity to posture and movement cues and its positive responses to approval in the form of praise and petting. More about this later when we look at the Social Dog.

TASTE

Dogs are not burdened with social values regarding what is or is not proper to put in their mouths, so just about anything that isn't burning gets tasted and often swallowed. This includes rotten meat, garbage, bugs, and that ultimate human No-No—stools (not the kind you sit on!). Though furniture, shoes, clothing, carpets and the like are also on their list of edibles in some cases, these nonfood items satisfy a psychologic rather than physical appetite.

Why a dog would ingest portions of its environment will be covered in later sections on Eating Nonfoods (pica) and Chewing. Stool-eating (coprophagia) is a separate subject, since it often involves health as well as psychologic problems. Suffice it to say a dog's sense of taste is probably as good as its sense of smell, and both can get a pet into trouble around the house.

Discriminating Taste

TOUCH

Touch (tactile) senses play a vital role in understanding behavior problems. Not only does *where* you touch a dog have basic meaning, but *how* you touch is important too.

Canine and human nervous systems are designed with one basic aim, the propagation of the species. To propagate, you must survive; to survive you need to get water and food, find shelter, avoid crippling injury or being devoured by another meat-eater, and to respond to sexual stimulation, performing the various gyrations required to propagate. Let's consider this vital tactile sense and some basic reflexes necessary to survival/propagation, as they relate to canine behavior problems.

An unexpected touch on the muzzle, head, neck or body (especially from the withers to the base of the skull) triggers a brain-stem reflex to bite. From an evolutionary view this is important. In the wild, even an instant's hesitation between touch and defensive action, such as turning to see if friend or foe has pounced, might result in serious injury or an unpleasant trip, as dinner, up a cliff to the lion's den.

Fortunately for us and our pets, nervous systems don't stop at the top of the spine with the brain stem. We both have more elaborate, higher brain centers that can control (inhibit) such basic reflexes. Without these, dogs or babies could never be housetrained.

Through gentle handling by persons, dogs learn to control the primitive defensive bite reflex and usually respond affectionately when touched, except when they are drowsy or asleep. Hence the old saying, "Let sleeping dogs lie," which unfortunately not all parents teach their children. This lack of training leads to thousands of dog bites every year and a trip to the pound for many innocent animals.

Another defensive reflex is activated when the paws or legs of the dog are touched, especially unexpectedly. The response is to withdraw the limb. This seems logical for survival, too, since withdrawal assures the dog's ability to take whatever action may be required, such as walking gingerly through a thorn patch.

These and other defensive reflexes we'll mention later occur in varying degrees in different dogs, even from the same litter of pups. Proper handling helps your pet learn to control them, but improper handling can actually strengthen them and confuse the dog.

For instance, knowledge of the touch-bite reflex ought to make clear how counterproductive it can be to swat a "mouthy" puppy across the snout. A more sensible correction would be to grab a paw and praise the pup when it stops mouthing due to the distraction created by the withdrawal reflex. This approach avoids the negative aspects that punishment can introduce to the relationship between owner and dog, while effectively correcting the problem. You will see how it is involved in several correction programs.

Courtship Behavior

People don't have a monopoly on foreplay before engaging in the ultimate intimacy of intercourse. In dogs it is called courtship behavior, with lots of tail-wagging, play-invitations and running together. It also involves a great deal of touching, especially nosing around the ears and neck, leaning on one another and, sometimes, putting the forepaws on the other's back.

It is interesting that almost every form of courtship behavior occurs within litters of puppies, well before puberty. Some pups respond to a human wrist or leg touching their throats or chests by firmly clasping their forelegs thereto, and performing vigorous pelvic thrusts. Most people don't abide this behavior, so they withdraw the stimulus and/or either scold or punish the puppy.

Fortunately, most dogs control their sex drives early among a human family. However, certain styles of petting by persons can

...nged petting can send a mixed message.

... the release of some basic hormones, and the dog ...an experience much frustration in keeping itself ...arking back to the role played by frustration in behavior problems, we'll be spending some time on the subject of petting in several later sections.

Pain

The sense of pain is closely associated with that of touch. Puppies raised in normal litters and transplanted to human families usually develop normal pain responses. But if a pup is raised in isolation from other living things, its pain perception can be severely hampered, along with other capabilities. For instance, when first exposed to an open flame, isolation-raised puppies may continually stick their noses into it, even until blisters appear. They also fail to avoid objects moving toward them, even though these cause pain to normally raised pups.

Given prolonged isolation, beyond three or four months of age, many pups develop a condition called *kennelosis*. Almost zombies, they barely react to anything. We'll look into this condition and how to avoid it in the Puppy section and the one on Shyness. For now, it is important to remember that dogs depend heavily on other living things for normal perceptive and emotional development.

DIRECTION

The sense of direction in dogs may not be as sharp as in homing pigeons, but it certainly beats that of man in most situations. Well-confirmed stories abound of dogs leading their hopelessly befuddled owners safely home through blinding snowstorms. Which sensory system makes these uncanny abilities possible is not known, but they can be troublesome during the housetraining of a puppy or older dog.

Dogs have to learn the route to their toilet area before you can deem them dependably housetrained. If they have to move north from the food bowl, turn west around the corner, then south to the back door, where it's west out the door and then north to the toilet area, a virtual maze-learning problem faces them. Since the first and final legs of the journey are northward, many undertrained dogs take a directional shortcut and wind up relieving themselves close to the north wall, but inside the house. This is as close as they can get to the toilet area using a canine compass. The Housetraining sections will deal with this problem.

BALANCE

A sense of balance keeps both people and dogs on their respective feet. Dogs can learn to walk tightropes and get about floors on either front or rear legs, alien as these feats are to the way they are built.

Balance is important in only one serious problem, that of carsickness. Even then the cause is more often emotional than physical.

There is one problem that balance can help in preventing or correcting, that of getting up on furniture. If you intend never to allow your pet this people-privilege, just move the furniture back and forward so as to upset the dog's balance when it jumps up. If you can do it so the dog doesn't realize you're the cause, so much the better. A few "unbalancing" sessions usually create a dependable floor-model dog.

EXTRASENSORY PERCEPTION

All animals have biological clocks, but pet dogs seem to develop an uncanny sense about when things like getting up, going for regular walks, feeding times and their owners' leaving and homecoming times are due to happen. In dogs, this sense has been scientifically shown to be accurate to within about 30 seconds in a 24-hour period.

This can be part of the cause for problems associated with being left alone or homecomings by owners when there is a lot of emotion attached to either. You'll see this element mentioned in all of the isolation-related problem corrections.

Extrasensory abilities are baffling enough when they occur in people, with whom they can be discussed. In our nonverbal dogs they are even more confounding. Problems may or may not be definitely related to ESP, but here is some food for thought concerning the dog's ability to anticipate storms and earthquakes, and to pick up on people's emotional states.

Some dogs start getting restless and exhibit whining or pacing hours or even days before thunderstorms or earthquakes occur. It is theorized that they somehow sense changes in humidity, barometric pressure or the positive-to-negative ratio of the air's ionization. Some dogs actually disappear well before clouds appear in the sky.

My case files indicate that the more fearful and/or hysterical a dog gets when the storm hits, the better are its forecasting abilities.

Correcting such dogs requires that their *first* feelings of fear be dealt with, and this may be hours or days before the actual storm hits.

You can find advice today that will tell you to get a phonograph record of thunderstorms, and create lightning to "fake" a storm, while getting the dog to sit or lie down calmly, at which time you give it praise or a tasty morsel. This approach assumes that dogs are too stupid to distinguish recordings and electronic flashes from the real thing, a fact not demonstrated in the real world of problem-solving. It further ignores our forecasting canine friends, who will be long gone or well into their frenzied panic by the time the thunder and lightning hit the scene.

As you will see, effective correction of behavior problems deals primarily with a pet dog's emotional perception of situations. Once this is changed, the actual behavior is quickly modified, sometimes by the dog itself, with no further effort on the owner's part.

Telepathy

A dog and owner lived with a close, healthy relationship for several years. The two were placed in separate rooms insulated from each other in every way scientifically known.

A burly man entered the owner's room and started menacing her. (She had not been forewarned of this part of the experiment.) The lady

was appropriately terrified. In its isolated room where it had formerly rested quietly, the dog became extremely nervous and upset, whining, pacing and seeking a way out.

This and other less scientific sorts of telepathic experiences abound in dog lore. Speculation as to how these occur ranges from "spiritual links," to undiscovered brain emanations that penetrate all known insulation methods and materials.

However it happens, most of us agree that our dogs somehow sense our underlying emotional states. As we proceed, you will see this dimension often is the key to understanding and then doing something about many behavior problems.

3

The Reflexive Dog

or

Why Dogs Fight, Take Flight, or Freeze

Reflexes are gifts from nature (inborn, or unconditioned) or the result of experience (learned or conditioned). Without reflexes we couldn't get up in the morning or swallow food. A textbook would be needed to describe all the dog's reflexes, so I will mention only those that bear on the development of problems or their correction.

PAVLOV AND CONDITIONED vs UNCONDITIONED REFLEXES

Years ago, a Russian investigator of reflexes, Ivan Pavlov, put dogs on tables, harnessed them securely and taught them various things, among which was to salivate when he rang a bell. The dogs quickly learned this trick because they were usually hungry when the experiments started, and were given food shortly after the bell rang.

Salivating for *food* is called an *unconditioned* (not learned) reflex, while drooling for the *bell* is a *conditioned* (learned) reflex. Pavlov's studies helped to classify reflexes in a way that is useful in understanding dog problems.

One thing Pavlov noticed was that all the dogs struggled, some mildly, some wildly, when they were first put into harness. So impressed was he about this reflex that he called it the "freedom reflex." The important thing about this reflex is that its strength tends to relate directly to how excitable the dog is. Excitability is a condition Pavlov attributed to the whole nervous system, especially the brain.

He measured it by testing how strongly dogs reacted to various stimuli. At the other end of the scale was how quickly dogs' nervous systems quit reacting to stimuli, which Pavlov called inhibition.

Pavlov's Principles

Though we may disagree with Pavlov's methods, one of which was to create grossly neurotic states, his studies did produce useful information.

Here are some of Pavlov's helpful findings:
- Excitable dogs are easier to upset emotionally and make neurotic.
- Excitable dogs go crazy actively, outwardly, a condition called "manic."
- Dogs with "balanced" nervous systems are more difficult to unbalance emotionally.
- Inhibited dogs are more difficult to make neurotic.
- Inhibited dogs react inwardly when they are emotionally unbalanced, becoming "depressed."

These principles should be kept in mind when you are selecting a pup or testing your own puppy with the handling test described in the Puppy Selection section. Which type gets along best in what type of environment is an important consideration in avoiding behavior problems.

Pavlov and his followers also documented many important things about how dogs learn. Here are two of those:
- Learned (conditioned) behavior requires six weeks of regular teaching before it tends to become permanent.
- Most dogs need to be taught in several different locations, with increasing distraction, before they can perform a task dependably.

This explains why your dog might sit nicely for you at home or in the yard, but seems to "go deaf" when you get to the veterinarian's office. Don't blame the dog, but teach it Sit in different places over six weeks, and you can solve the problem.

DEFENSE REFLEXES

Defense reflexes become evident when the dog perceives a threat to its well-being. It is important to understand that all of us and our pets possess an ultimate expression of defensive behavior that *will* surface when faced with physical harm. This natural endowment is not a

"Up, Boy! Up on the table! Up, I say! Up! He does it at home! Up! Dumb! Up! Up!"

character flaw in man or animal. It is merely a fact of life. Faced with a threat, a dog will either *Fight,* take *Flight,* or *Freeze.*

If you decide physical punishment is the way to correct undesirable behavior, and your dog is a passive, freeze-type, it will probably require only the mildest sign of physical threat to get your point across. A flight-type will retreat, but will probably bite if held or cornered for punishment. The fight-type may tolerate a certain amount of harsh treatment, but beware! Nature will out, and sooner or later you may need to settle the issue with a club, or admit defeat and hie yourself off to the emergency ward for some expensive stitchery.

On the other hand (and unfortunately) many fight-type dogs will suppress their active-aggressive defense tendencies with you, but will not do so when someone else (often a family child) makes what the dog *perceives* as a menacing move. This can result in an injured child and a dead pet dog, victimized by its basic nature, human ignorance and the ultimate solution, euthanasia.

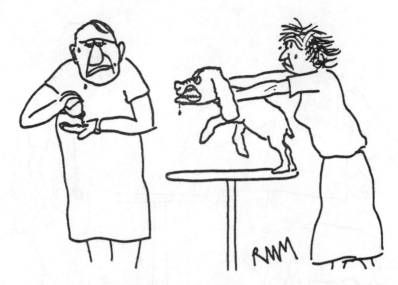

"Give her one tranquilizing tablet before guests arrive, two before riding in the car, and eight before she comes to me again."

I have helped hundreds of owners achieve satisfying lives with such dogs, with never a sign of such misplaced aggression, simply by working with the *causes* of problems rather than punishing the symptoms. I will continue to stress the comparative futility of physical punishment, in the hope of preventing some of the heartbreaks it can create.

Defensive Biting

We have already considered the bite and withdrawal reflexes associated with the tactile senses of the head, body and legs. A bite can also be suffered when ill-advised folks blow into a dog's ear. A dog will even bite a bicycle pump used for this purpose.

Many little human faces are scarred every year because children hug dogs around the neck and innocently exhale a gleeful puff into the pet's ear. Most dogs learn to inhibit this bite reflex, but the best policy is child-training against breathing into any dog's ears, even the most docile.

Anything moving quickly into a dog's field of vision will also stimulate a defensive bite reflex, which probably accounts for most of the oral bee stings dogs suffer. Just as a human baby grabs with its hand things that suddenly appear, so we adults will instinctively (inborn-reflexively) catch a ball unexpectedly tossed to us. Unfortunately, the dog's equipment for catching things is full of teeth and many a well-meaning person gets nipped while reaching to exchange a little affection with the new puppy. This sort of negative feedback can lead to severe punishment for the pup, unless the owner is enlightened.

Corrective Measures

Mouthy, biting pups and even older dogs with overactive visual bite reflexes can be corrected effectively without resorting to sticking your fingers or fist down the animal's throat, squeezing its lips against its teeth, hitting it, or otherwise causing pain, any of which risk stimulating more aggression. Using the "brains beats brawn" approach leads to permanent nonpainful correction. Such techniques as the grab-a-paw method mentioned in Chapter 2, or petting the chest and throat with your other hand as you reach into the dog's visual field are effective "touch distractions."

Persistent, rambunctious, mouthy pups or small breeds usually become manageable if you gently roll them onto their backs and hold them still until they calm down. This "restraint-dominance" technique is shown in the Puppy Selection Test section.

I mention these defensive biting reflexes only as they relate to mouthy pups and small breeds. But if you have a pet that bites with *intent* (not just simple reflex reactions) or is angry or fearful, DO NOT try to roll it onto its back and hold it down or use the foot-grab or pet-on-the-chest routines; you could get bitten! Emotionally based (not reflexive) problems demand emotionally based corrections, which I will present later.

Having looked at the simple defensive bite reflexes, let's take a look at the overall canine nervous system and see how it's wired for reflexes, both inborn and learned, and how a dog's general excitability (nervousness) affects behavior problems and their corrections.

THE ORIENTING REFLEX

When we considered the Sensitive (Perceptive) Dog in Chapter 2 we mentioned what sorts of things were perceived, and what reflexes and other responses were stimulated, to present a meaningful picture of the subject as it relates to behavior problems. We will take a similar approach to the Reflexive Dog. It will be of little use to say that the orienting reflex serves to alert your dog to changes in the environ-

The orienting reflex alerts the dog to life's hazards.

ment, unless I describe the types of things that trigger the reflex, what effect it has on the dog's mental processes and how it can take part in causing or correcting behavior problems.

Man, dogs and all other normal mammals share a life-preserving orienting reflex. It operates through all our senses to let us know something outside, on, or even inside our bodies has changed. A simpler name for it might be the "What's that?" reflex.

The effect of this reflex is an extremely brief interruption of ongoing mental activity and, in the case of an outside-the-body change, attention (orienting) toward the source of the change, or *stimulus*. Without the orienting reflex we wouldn't notice dangerous things like approaching cars until we felt the crunch of collision.

Immediately following the orienting reflex comes the mental process of locating and interpreting the nature of the change (stimulus) so a decision can be made as to whether or not to do something about it, such as putting on the brakes and steering clear of a collision.

The sensitivity of the orienting reflex depends on our degree of awakeness. It is nearly dormant when we slumber, so a very strong stimulus is required to trigger it. On the other hand, when we are "wound up" about things, intent or expectant, even a very weak stimulus (like someone lightly touching a shoulder) can startle us, and a strong stimulus can cause our hearts to skip a beat or two.

With their sharp senses, dogs are especially reactive to their orienting reflexes, which gives us a marvelous tool for teaching simple things like Come, Sit and Stay, without leashes or the need to touch them—as you'll see in the Puppy Training section. More important, though, is the way the orienting reflex opens an avenue to our dogs' emotions, since it is followed by the *locating, interpreting* and *deciding* processes mentioned earlier. If I can show you how to affect and change the way your dog *feels* about things, you'll have the secret to solving even severe problems. Let's take a case and see how it works.

Aggressive Behavior

You have a dog that shows extreme aggression toward people arriving at the house. It has bitten one visitor. We won't consider now how this problem developed, only what you have done to try to control it.

You started by holding the dog's collar, petting and trying to speak soothingly to reassure the dog, which didn't work. So you tried the negative-feedback routines: you scolded, spanked, put it on a leash, and now you've reached the point where you put the dog out or in a separate room when folks come to call.

All of these steps have failed for the following reasons: The petting and reassuring tones were interpreted by the dog as approval of its aggressive behavior and feelings of hostility, so things got worse due to *positive reinforcement*. The heavy-handed stuff failed because the dog associated the arrivals with nonpleasurable treatment from you, ending with the ultimate disgrace of being excluded from the "pack"—all *negative reinforcements*.

The situation has gotten so bad that your dog now starts barking and charging the door when it hears footsteps out front, or when a car door slams. Using our chain of events that starts with the orienting reflex to the car door or footsteps, your pet gets as enraged at those noises as it used to get when face-to-face with the terrified visitors. To make matters even more complicated, the dog has started growling at you when you grab its collar to take it to the other room or outdoors. Now you're afraid *you* may get bitten!

The Interpretive Factor
The ways you taught your dog to interpret the arrival of visitors—petting and trying to reassure, then angry scolding, punishment and social rejection—all innocently reinforced its hostile emotions.

AGGRESSION TOWARDS VISITORS:

CAUSE

EFFECT

Things might have been better if you had sat down and cried about the situation! At least crying would have provided the dog with a different emotional interpretation of the situation, a process which I call the *interpretive factor*. So, now what to do?

Since your pet's nasty behavior is a result of its feelings of hostility, the solution lies in changing its emotional interpretation of the situation. This occurs well before it is facing folks at the door, as we've seen.

By the way, you also have one vitally important emotional element in favor of correcting your problem. Your dog *loves* to play ball about as much as it *hates* the arrival of visitors. This will be important when using the orienting reflex and interpretive factor.

Here is the sequence of events in a "set-up" situation to correct this behavior:

- Footsteps occur; dog alerts; footsteps instantly stop.
- Instantly after dog alerts, you clap hands, bounce ball, happily move about and invite dog to play, until it takes part. (The hand-clap and ball-bounce cause a second orienting reflex, which interrupts the dog's initiation of hostility. The happy movement and upbeat invitation provide a new interpretive factor—one of jollity.)

The Jolly Routine

The Jolly Routine

This whole procedure is called the Jolly Routine. It will be used in correcting most of the serious, emotionally based problems, including fearfulness.

As you will see later, the Jolly Routine must be applied while gradually bringing the footsteps closer to the house, until finally the guests arrive at the door to take part in the ball game.

WARNING: We will also find there is much more to correcting aggressive behavior than merely applying this routine, which alone could result in possible disaster. First you'll need to gain a position of *emotional leadership* with your dog. Otherwise you could be running around bouncing the ball while your dog is trying to tear the front door off its hinges! More about this later. Now, on to more reflexes.

THE CHASE REFLEX

The chase reflex appears almost as soon as pups are able to move around on all fours. Anything that moves fast is doomed to get pursued and pounced upon. This may be invaluable for developing prey-catching skills in the wild, but it gets downright exasperating when practiced on human ankles and clothing around the house. It becomes genuinely vexing when it graduates outdoors and is aimed at bicycles, cars and running people.

This predatory, game-chasing reflex does not have an emotional base in most cases, and it requires extra portions of patience, effort and time for correction, as will be seen in the Chasing section.

THE "PUSH-BACK" REFLEX

Numerous reflexes combine to keep a dog's body in any particular position—standing, sitting, lying down, or in any stage of movement. One that is useful with problem dogs and for teaching certain things is called *thigmotaxis,* or the "push-back" reflex. You can test it in your dog by gently pressing against the side of its rump while it is standing. That pressure pushing back at you is caused by *positive* thigmotaxis. If instead of pushing back the dog gives way, you have stimulated *negative* thigmotaxis, a rare response except in dogs having severely inhibited nervous systems or those suffering from kennelosis due to isolation from normal social contacts during puppyhood.

Understanding the push-back reflex helps avoid and solve some problems. For instance, the best way to stop a pesky dog from leaning

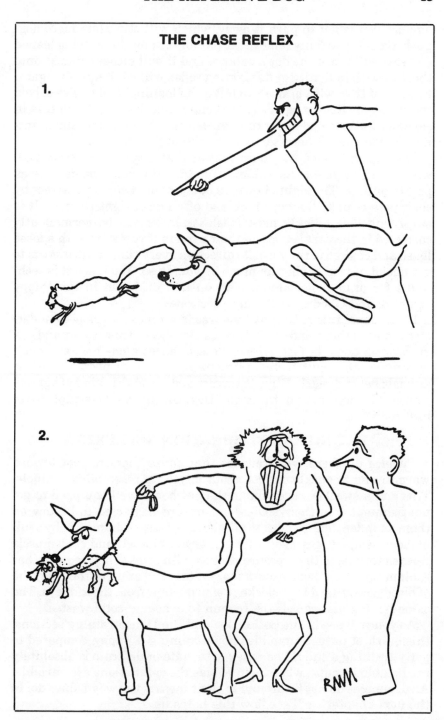

against you is not to push it away, which will stimulate more dog-push. Rather, suddenly remove the part of your anatomy being leaned on. This will upset the dog's balance and it will either collapse onto the floor with indignity, or its righting reflex will jolt it upright again. Enough of this, with praise when it quits leaning, and you've solved the problem. Remember Pavlov, though, and be sure to do this in several locations and every time the leaning occurs. One "unbalancing" lesson doesn't necessarily solve the problem.

This reflex is also the main reason that dogs make great sled, wagon and bicycle pullers. Unfortunately, the same holds true as people-pullers. The sight of owners being hauled down the street by their pets is incredibly common and often downright comical. It is surprising how quickly most leash-strainers can be permanently corrected in the early stages of their careers if you start with a loose leash and change to the opposite direction every time the dog *starts* to get ahead of you, saying its name as you do so. You'll see this technique for animal leadership both on and off leash in the Puppy Training and Obedience Training sections.

If we couple this reflex with the freedom reflex, it's easy to understand how tethers and tight leashes can cause frustration and aggression in dogs. In fact, for some dogs, fences alone create enough frustration to result in severe aggression toward people or other animals beyond reach. Ways to correct and avoid this kind of aggression will be presented in the Social Dog, Biting, and Overprotectiveness sections.

EATING AND ELIMINATION REFLEXES

Puppies are born with reflexes that cause them to root toward warmth and to suckle on just about anything resembling a nipple. This and a swallow reflex make the newborns well equipped to get nourishment into their bodies, but nature neglected to bestow on them an independent reflex to eliminate wastes. A human baby's full bladder sends a message to its urinary sphincter, and that muscle relaxes to relieve the pressure. Not so with pups. They require that their mother lick them around the genitals and anus, or they may die of blood poisoning due to blockage of urine flow from the kidneys. The same licking also causes the rectum to evacuate solid wastes.

As you will see in the Social Dog and the Housetraining sections, this quirk of nature simplifies housetraining a puppy, compared to potty-training a child. The reflex to urinate or defecate is absolutely predictable in pups, whereas in babies these functions are variable. Also, puppies do not lie around in their messes the way babies do. In the next chapter we'll see how this helps us.

4

The Social Dog

or

Forever a Teenager

All domestic puppies can transfer their social tendencies from their own to the human pack. This is possible because of built-in reactions that appear shortly after birth. Let's look at some that can lead to problems as well as form the basis for corrections.

LIFE IN THE LITTER

Mother Nature—Housetraining Helper

Unlike human babies, puppies do not arrive with an independent physical mechanism for urinating or defecating. As mentioned previously, if their dam did not roll them onto their side or back and lick their genitals and anus to cause urination and defecation, the pups would soon die from the toxic effects of backed-up urine.

After the roll-and-lick ritual, the good mother laps up the urine and eats the fecal material. This may seem disgusting, but healthy puppy waste is sterile, and this routine guarantees litter hygiene. It also creates a great mechanism for later housetraining, since the little ones develop a reflex habit of evacuating their waste matter shortly after eating or drinking. You'll find this reflex at work in the Housetraining section for both pups and adult dogs.

Submissive Signals

Another reflex response to the mother's licking occurs as she cleans up about the youngsters' faces and throats; they raise their forepaws

as if trying to fend off the attacking tongue. As she persists, most pups give up the battle and draw their forelegs into the sides of their chests in a kind of clasped pocket-knife position. Some even urinate. You can see both of these submissive responses in some adult dogs. A mild form occurs when a dog sits and raises a bent foreleg.

In the litter situation, the pups have experienced exposure to their first *dominance* as the dam rolled them over for clean-up. Though appearing to object to some degree, the puppies have for the first time displayed *submission* as a behavioral response.

Suckling and Swallowing Reflexes

Two other built-in reflexes are to suckle when hungry, and to swallow when the suckled matter gets to a certain place in the mouth. Just like a human infant, a pup will try to get anything small enough into its mouth and give it a good working over. The reflex to root after anything warm and soft generally leads the pup to a nipple and nourishment. If it happens to get attached to a littermate's tail or foot, the mother will usually pull the errant puppy to the proper place.

As the pups mature, their rooting and suckling reflexes fade, usually during the weaning stage. However, some adult dogs will suckle on blankets, clothing and even their owners when they appear to feel emotionally insecure.

"Kissing" for Dinner

The weaning process begins about four weeks after birth. Many breeders force this process by taking the dam away from her litter. They provide soft food, usually in a large tray, at the time when the pups' eyesight is developing through a blurry stage, so they are able to waddle to dinner.

Other litters are naturally weaned, and the mother will often start to regurgitate some of her own food, which the young gobble up. After a couple of these experiences, the pups begin to lick the dam around her mouth when she finishes her own meal, and she vomits in response.

Keep this in mind when a cuddly ball of canine fur licks at your face. You could be mistaking affection for a request to throw up! Lots of people encourage face-licking by rewarding it with petting and praise. Then, when the maturing or adult dog jumps up to get a little "love and kisses," it gets scolded or punished, a prime example of changing the rules and creating potential problems.

Chewing—Gratuitous and Otherwise

With the transfer to more substantial food, suckling and licking fade and are replaced with picking up food by lapping with the tongue or grabbing it in the jaws, followed by the swallowing reflex mentioned earlier.

In the wild state, wolves and dogs start earning their nourishment early, between about six and twelve weeks of age. They earn it in the sense that they must do a lot of ripping and chewing at prey animals killed by older pack members. This may serve a dual purpose: priming young noses and taste buds for their natural prey, and developing tremendously strong jaw muscles that eventually will crush many spines for survival.

Pet puppies do not go through this chew-for-food stage, but usually gain strong jaws anyway. We give them various chewable toys to help

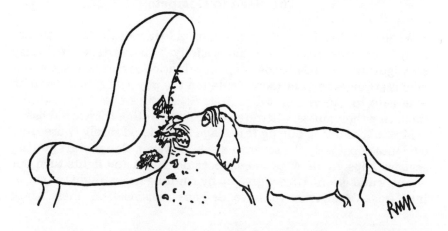

them through the teething stage, with the hope that this will also keep them from trying to devour valuable portions of the household environment. None of this toy-chewing relates to filling their bellies, so this oral activity becomes a pastime, a sort of hobby. And being great fun, it also becomes generalized to the rest of the environment, with almost anything becoming fair game—shoes, furniture, carpets—you name it!

Fortunately, chewing problems are basically related to tension-relieving behavior, so there are solutions and ways to minimize the damage. In the meantime we can hope for the day that dog food will be sold in tough, edible containers that will keep our pets busy chewing-for-chow up to a half an hour, rather than the few seconds it takes to gulp down the pap and kibbles currently on the market.

GROWING UP

The Need to Follow

A fascinating and useful behavior shows up as the pup develops eyesight sharp enough to see things moving at a distance from the litter; it follows the moving object. Just what is moving doesn't seem to matter. It can be a mechanical toy, littermate, its mother or a person.

Even if you isolate a puppy from seeing moving things until it is several months old, it will engage in this following response, which forms the basis for all its later development of social bonds. The response will also be an indispensable part of both the development and correction of behavior problems, as we will see.

The Need to Compete

When pups are four to seven weeks old they begin to get things sorted out between one another socially. This starts with clumsy playfighting, which helps develop coordination and experience about who is strongest and/or more skilled in the physical arts, as well as who gets to the dinner table first. Some pups even try sexually mounting their mates, with no obvious motive other than to be bossy.

Most of the biting during this stage is mild and rarely causes any evidence of pain. By the seventh week, however, things start getting serious. Nips get painful, growls become snarls and fights turn out winners and losers. Losers give up by running away (flight) or showing "freeze" behavior (passive defense response). Winners stalk

Top Dog

around picking fights until they get whipped into submissive behavior themselves, meet their equal and declare a truce, or wind up "top dog."

Meanwhile, in the loser's bracket, further sorting out takes place to determine where on the social ladder each pup will rank.

The Social Ladder

It is important to understand that puppies, even the most submissive ones, are capable of acting dominantly, and that the most bossy, dominant of them can display submissive behavior, depending on the circumstances. In an eight-puppy litter, the #3 pup will act submissively to #1 when it approaches dominantly. A little later, #3 will look like a #1 when it dominates pup #7 in the hierarchy.

It is also vital to keep in mind that these displays are refined into very subtle signals as the litter matures. In the early stages, a dominant dog may have to pounce and pin an underling to prove its point. After awhile, merely staring can cause a subordinate to lower its tail and head and look away, signalling submission.

Another example occurs when the dominant pup approaches, tail up, ears forward and places its muzzle over the subordinate's head or shoulders. The underling may stand still, lower its head and tail, even growl as it raises its lips in a kind of smile. Boss pups learn to recognize this as part of the canine submissive ritual so long as the other doesn't make a wrong move.

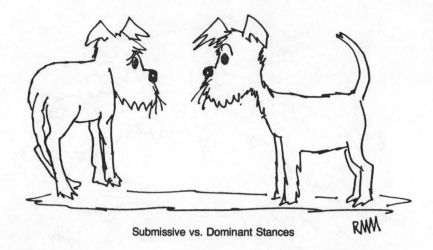

Submissive vs. Dominant Stances

All this serves nicely to keep domestic puppies from injuring each other while among the litter, which is as far as most of them will mature while still intimately coexisting with their own kind. In wolves and wild dogs, however, dominance and submission rituals will determine which animals eat first and get the best and most of the prey, as well as which ones breed. Both of these rituals play important roles in the survival of the fittest and propagation of the species.

Not so with our pet dogs, whose matings are either accidental or based on physical appearance, and whose food is amply provided under noncompetitive conditions. In this sense, while their wild cousins will mature as cooperating members of functional packs, our pets are doomed to lifelong emotional and functional adolescence. They are fed when hungry, supplied with water, washed and groomed when dirty, walked or given outdoor access when needed or asked for, petted and stroked when they nudge for it (or just because they are cute) and given medical attention when required. With us waiting on their every need and responding to nearly every whim, is it any wonder our puppies grow up feeling they are the *leaders* in our relationships?

The Critical Seventh Week

Let's examine some of the basic differences between pups as they relate to littermates and to people at that critical period around the seventh week of life, when they usually make the transition to a human household.

Years ago I demonstrated part of the Puppy Selection Test (page 114) for CBS-TV in Los Angeles. We carefully observed a litter of seven-week-old Golden Retrievers, identifying the dominant litter boss and the lowest ranking pup. As I entered the litter enclosure the dominant pup led the group to jump up and greet me, while the most submissive, bottom-ranked (also smallest) hung back timidly.

I picked up the boss and gently carried him to an area away from the sight and sound of the litter, placed him on the ground, walked away, crouched down and beckoned to him, softly clapping my hands. Cautiously, tail down, he approached me. When he arrived, I gently rolled him onto his back and held him with one hand on his breastbone. He froze. When 30 seconds had passed I released the puppy and placed him in a sitting position at my feet. The "boss-dog" then proceeded to urinate on my shoe, much to the glee of the TV crew, who were using a close-up lens! I picked up the puppy, praising and petting it on the trip back to the litter, placed him down back "home," and he immediately started picking on the nearest littermate.

You've probably already guessed what happened with the submissive litter runt, but just to confirm your hunch, I'll relate the scene. Tail up, she resisted my invitation to come, bit at my hand, flailed and scratched when I held her in the submissive roll-over and tried again to bite me when I put her in a sitting position to pet her.

This phenomenon, with some exceptions and variations, bears out the contention that puppies do not necessarily perceive persons as they do other dogs, but react uniquely to each. It also points out the difference between rituals of dominance and the ultimate defense reflexes to fight, take flight or freeze.

This is the reason you will find the Puppy Selection Test valuable in deciding which pup from among an adorable litter will best fit into your scheme of things. It will also help to avoid any behavioral surprises when you arrive home with your choice.

Reaction to Threat

A pup or an older dog may react to perceived threats to its well-being by acting submissively, in an effort to convey the idea, "OK, I give up. Please don't hurt me." If we recognize this, we should further realize that to press the animal with more severe threats or painful punishment amounts to changing the rules of the game. This can create enough perceived threat to cause the dog to react according to its basic defensive nature. The result may be a pet that is a submissive wetter, a runaway, a fear-biter, or an aggresssive beast.

Eye Contact

I have already mentioned the effect of eye contact between dominant and submissive littermates. From your own point of view, it can create problems to try to establish dominance by staring unwaveringly at your own or other pets. Long-distance challenges invite hostility where friendliness ought to exist.

Training for Fighting

When pups are kept together as a litter through the ninth week or so, serious trouble can break out. Bully-types get more so; midrankers vie with greater intensity, and all may turn on an especially submissive puppy and injure or kill it. For these and other reasons yet to be mentioned, it is wise to obtain new puppies at between 6 and 8 weeks of age.

Observing the litter for about an hour before and during feeding time can be educational. If there is serious aggression between puppies, and you dislike breaking up dog fights, it is a good idea to move on and look at another, more peaceful group.

Exceptions to the Rule

The seven-week principle for the puppy's transition from canine to human companionship does not mean a behavioral tragedy will occur should you get yours earlier or later. Fortunately, many breeders expose their litters to socialization before, during and after the so-called best age. If this has been the practice, it will make itself clear to you in the behavior of older litters, especially if you use the Puppy Selection Test (page 114).

THE PUPPY IN THE HUMAN FAMILY

The most important single social characteristic of a pet dog has a Greek tongue-twister for a name: *allelomimetic* behavior, which literally means behavior that is "of one another imitative." *Allelo* comes from genetics, and *mimetic* was tacked on by someone studying genetics and behavior.

The simplest form of this trait common to all social animals can be seen when schools of fish or flocks of flying birds move and change direction as if they were one. Puppies show it when they all flock happily toward somebody entering the litter area, if they have been properly socialized toward people. On the other hand, I have seen unsocialized and poorly socialized litters show fearful, extremely timid or downright hostile reactions when people entered their domain.

The important difference between dogs and other allelomimetic animals is that dogs raised in human families will take their cues from people. Our pet dogs reinforce our own emotional expressions of happiness and affection; they run when we run, show concern when we are distraught, even share many of our hostilities. Otherwise we might keep them in cages as things of beauty, or perhaps cook them for dinner, as is the case in several cultures even today.

And yet, ironically, the very things that create our close social bonds also lead to most of the behavior problems we will be discuss-

"Has he been watching an awful lot of TV?"

Some dogs are more allelomimetic than others.

ing. If we deny this emotional aspect of our pet relationships, I might as well be writing a book about techniques to train circus animals. However, there are lots of these books already available, many of them disguised as behavioral guides for dog owners. The *causative* approach to problem behavior depends on understanding the emotional aspects of dog ownership.

The Need to Investigate

An appealing but troublemaking behavior that begins blossoming at about six weeks of age is to look at, smell, paw at, chew and taste nearly everything in the environment. When you remember that at the same age the eyesight of puppies is getting keener all the time, it is no wonder they are always in hot water if left alone around the house. This intense investigating recedes with experience and time, but without proper guidance it can create major problems later. The Puppy section presents ways of minimizing household mayhem and still satisfying a pup's natural curiosity during this stage.

The Need to Fear

As a pup approaches ten weeks of age there is a period wherein certain events can produce lifelong fear responses. Not only that, but other things associated with those fear-producing elements can become *conditioned* fear-stimulators. This can be used to advantage for teaching a pup to avoid venturing into streets on its own, if the lesson is supervised carefully. But it can produce behavior problems based on unreasonable fears, or phobias, about being left alone.

Let's say a puppy yipped and wailed when left alone in the kitchen or laundry room on its first night in a new home during this fear period. Its behavior was absolutely normal, but the new owner wanted to get some sleep. He had read somewhere that "natural" punishment for puppies is to grab them by the scruff of the neck and shake them. The owner didn't recall (if the book or article even mentioned it) how hard to shake, what pup-response to look for, what type of nervous system could or could not take such punishment, or what type of defense reflexes might be most amenable to the shake-down routine. So, he just started shaking, and the puppy started screaming bloody murder—another natural response. So he shook harder, which stimulated the pup to higher and louder vocal accomplishments. Violent shaking finally stifled the puppy, who settled for soft whimpers and sought to get physically close to its new owner.

The owner also had read that praise for stopping unwanted behavior was needed. So he picked up and cuddled the pup, told him what a good dog he was, placed him back in his box, closed the door and went to bed for an uninterrupted night's sleep.

Now, if we hark back to the puppy's social, reflexive and defensive properties, even ignoring the fear-response period, we can see the possible dangers in this type of approach. Some of the subsequent problems are obvious: submissive wetting in the presence of the man who punished it; extreme anxiety when left alone, resulting in tension-relieving, destructive chewing; difficulty in housetraining; and biting the family children when they attempted to correct the dog at 6 months of age.

The foregoing are not just possibilities. I am relating a client's actual case history. More than one night's traumatic encounter was needed to produce the adult fear-biter I met after its veterinarian referred the case. However, it's a classic example of how early mismanagement sows the seeds for problems later.

I should also mention that the same treatment of a more resilient pup may not provide a foundation for problems. However, there are more reasonable, satisfying and humane methods, and it seems shortsighted not to use them. A different approach is presented in Chapter 6.

The Mythical Need for Sex

At about twelve weeks of age, puppies start going through puberty. They begin sexually mounting both living and inanimate things. If there was ever an area of behavior where projecting human feelings to animals is valid, this is it. Masturbation is its own reward. However, doing it in public is a No-No for which human beings are often sent to mental institutions or jail, if they persist. So the sight of a puppy unabashedly humping away on a blanket or somebody's foot usually stimulates instant, negative human feedback, based on human moral standards of conduct.

I have seen both male and female dogs, neutered and intact, with serious aggressive problems, whose owners have either tolerated or encouraged their pet's misdirected amorous behavior. At the other extreme, overly harsh physical punishment has led to the very same type of problems. This paradox might be due to aggressive tendencies that develop at about the same age.

Whatever may be the cause, the best method for correction is to use the orienting reflex to interrupt the mental fix on the activity and instantly redirect the pup's attentions to some play activity, such as chasing a ball. This avoids the excesses of either permissiveness or punishment.

If the distract-to-play routine is used, even the most humpy pups hold their sexual expressions in check in short order. Luckily, most

"That's what I wanted to ask you about."

properly raised puppies seem to mature through this stage in a couple of months.

The Need to Dream

From all outward appearances, puppies dream quite a bit. Just like people, their eyes move vigorously in a stage of sleep called Rapid Eye Movement (REM). If you wake a person every time his eyeballs start gyrating, you can cause all sorts of emotional and behavioral abnormalities, including signs of neurosis and psychosis, and hallucinations.

Depriving a pup or mature dog of its REM sleep has produced some of the most bizarre canine behavior I have ever seen. The explanation given by the owners was that the pet seemed to be having terrible nightmares, and that waking it seemed the humane thing to do.

Back when I used to make housecalls, I entered the apartment of a young couple whose seven-month-old female Fox Terrier had been described as "irrepressively unruly." Seeing no dog, I asked where she was.

"In the closet." came the unison reply.

I suggested we let her out, but the lady said, "Before we do, I want you to know that if you can't help us we're going to have to get rid of her. John hasn't had a good night's rest in five months."

If you guessed that John had been waking the dog every time it whined during a dream, you've almost got the picture. In fact, John had also been sleeping on the floor with Foxie for the past three months!

When the closet door was opened, a canine behavioral cyclone hit the room. Foxie jumped up at us, raced around bumping into furniture and walls, barked incessantly and was impossible to control. Before 45 minutes passed, she wore herself out and went to sleep on the sofa beside me.

I whispered my advice that John rejoin his bride in bed at night and stay there. Even if Foxie's dream-state whimpering woke him, he was advised to let her work it out herself. Five days later he phoned to say what a great dog they had. She even stopped chewing and barking when they left her alone.

Other canine problems apparently caused by people who interfere with the privacy of their pet's dreams range from self-mutilation to dog-fights and biting.

The Need to Fight

For most domestic pups there is no need to learn the canine martial arts. However, at around 13 weeks of age most of them act as if there were. Among other dogs they will engage in long playfighting sessions until exhausted. Unless anger sets in, I have not seen problems I could blame on the activity. However, when play turns to anger, it is best to break it up by distracting the dogs without getting angry yourself. Scolding or punishing either dog risks conveying the idea that you are taking sides in the dispute, which can increase the chances for more serious fighting later.

Given no other animals on which to exercise their playful fighting tendencies, most puppies will either invite, or respond to, playfighting with their two-legged pack members. This can teach a most unfortunate lesson; the pet learns to *contest* its people with physical force, which usually includes its jaws. Worse yet, if the puppy gets angry during the fracas, it has also learned to lose its temper with people and put some real meaning into its bites. The possible consequences of this are clear; either the human fighter backs off or applies more force until the animal shows submission.

"Do human beings get ear mites, Doctor?"

Following advice to "act like a dog" to solve behavior problems can produce unwanted side effects.

Canine horseplay has a role in wild packs, where it seems to help keep the group together. In fact, in many wild and domestic dog playfights the dominant animal rolls over, allowing a subordinate to take the dominant role. The reason for this exchange isn't clear, and until some talking dog explains it to us, the wisest policy is to let it remain their secret. Bringing to mind the dog's various sensory capabilities and our limitations, people would probably make poor dog-pack members, and trying to act like one isn't nearly as easy as getting dogs to act like people.

The Need to Defend the Pack/Family

Territorial and group defense behavior also starts showing itself in the early juvenile period. Strangers and known visitors who formerly had been gleefully welcomed are now often approached cautiously, sometimes aggressively, or even fearfully avoided.

These changes could be the result of the pup's improving eyesight which, at about this age, allows it to discriminate at a distance between family folks and outsiders. Lots of people who get dogs with protection in mind are delighted to see their pups bark and show aggression, so they encourage it wholeheartedly. This can be as ill-advised as is the practice of trying to reassure a puppy by petting it and saying things like, "It's OK, Tuffy."

Both of these actions positively reinforce the pup's aggressive feelings and behavior at a time when it needs to be taught to discriminate between friend and foe.

Discriminate between friend and foe.

People who do not want an aggressive defender also make a mistake when they scold or punish this behavior. This kind of negative reinforcement can teach the pup to feel hostile toward visitors.

Whatever the pup's behavior, the best bet for avoiding problems and teaching dependable watchdog behavior is to teach through leadership. If it is a friend or nonthreatening person approaching, show the pup by approaching the person and standing alongside or walking with him or her into the house, paying little or no attention to the puppy. This allows your dog to interpret the situation as you do.

On the other hand, if you are unsure about the visitor, do what comes naturally and act that way. Your pup will likely do the same, thereby learning from your example to recognize the contrast between situations calling for wariness or friendliness.

Territorial Marking

As long as we are on the subject of pack and territory, the need to brand things with urine or defecation rates some attention, although it develops later on, at five months of age or older.

Objectively, domestic dogs don't really *need* to carve out and hold a wide hunting territory through scent-mark stations to scare off competing predators. They also do not need to roll in rotten carcasses or feces. Even without the need, most pet dogs seem to *want* to perform one or more of these practices. It is as if the scent of another dog's urine, the approach of another animal or a feeling of threat or insecurity about the pack or its territory arouses the need to lay a brand on things.

One way to help cause problems such as chasing vehicles and people, dog- and cat-fighting, escaping, running away, excessive yard-barking, household urine and/or defecation marking, and even aggression toward people, is to allow your dog to place its canine "Mark of Zorro" beyond its own legal territory. To do so creates a desire on the dog's part to return and freshen up its scent posts. Unless it can be done routinely, sometimes daily, this can cause frustration. If it is allowed too frequently, the dog may begin defending the territory in ways too primitive for acceptable pet-behavior, such as the aggressiveness mentioned earlier.

Some dogs will even urinate on their own pack members when they feel some threat to their relationship. This way of saying, "You belong to me," as well as leaving urine or feces on an owner's pillow or other belongings, may make a dog feel better, but people tend to regard it as downright insulting. Correction usually entails more than putting a stop to the nightly neighborhood walk, as you will see.

Mark of ownership.

The Need to Vocalize

Pups start making noises very shortly after they are born. These are associated with hunger, pain, being too hot or cold, feeling abandoned, or even feeling content.

As they move about and mix things up physically, growling, snarling, yipping and yowling are added to the repertoire. Barking starts at various ages and, when it first occurs, most pups appear perplexed, as if wondering where the noise came from. Depending on the feedback they get, pups usually either do a lot of barking, or very little. For instance, if they are among a litter that has reasons for lots of barking, most of the individual pups will tend to be "barky."

In a human home, barky dogs can create problems. Also, quiet dogs can be made into barkers through innocent reinforcement by people.

Howling as an expression of loneliness or in response to the odor of a distant bitch in heat is heard most often in breeds from the northern climes. However, once one dog in an area starts it, many others get the urge to join the chorus.

If your pup is prone to vocal expression and you want to nurture a problem, just encourage it a little. The sections on Whining and Barking deal with avoiding and correcting vocal problems.

The Need to Lead

With very few exceptions, the problem dogs and their people I have consulted with for almost twenty years have been vying for leadership. When I get called into this game the dog is usually ahead. It has the owners backed into a corner, so attached emotionally they can't kick the animal out of the house or take it to the pound or veterinarian for euthanasia. The thought of giving it away is unbearable. On an intellectual level the owners have exhausted all the means known to them for correcting their delinquent, and they are reduced to seeking outside guidance.

Even though well in front on the scoreboard, the dogs act as if they don't know it. They keep the contest at near fever-pitch, letting me know from the moment we meet just who is in charge in no uncertain canine terms. Here's how they do it.

When the family car is safely stopped in the consultation area, the door opens, and the dog bursts out ahead of everyone. Either that or it

"So that night, after you ordered no more table scraps, we were eating a steak dinner, and Flash sat up and begged, and I said, 'No, Flash . . .'"

has to be commanded to Stay or physically held back. Nice bossy dogs approach me and jump and tell me to pet them. Nasty ones stalk around, hike a leg on my walnut tree, show me some raised hackles, circle me, or outright charge me to say I'd better not interfere with their "boss" position.

When the owners and I head for the office door, guess who's there first? If the owner opens it, the dog barges through. When we are inside and I ask the owner to get up as if to leave, no degree of human speed can beat Bowser to the threshold. It requires another command or some unreasonable physical punishment if the owner is going to score any points in this part of the leadership game.

I have seen this so often, with both super-submissive and dangerously dominant dogs, that it is almost totally predictable. I have seen it in relationships where the dog was extremely submissive to the owner, and others where the dog had ripped up an owner for simply using a threatening tone of voice.

Just who is dominant does not seem to be the deciding factor in most dog behavior problems. Rather, who *thinks* or *feels* he or she should be leading in the relationship decides the issue. Unfortunately, when the pet dog feels the burden of leadership, it must inevitably meet with frustration and suffer the anxieties and tensions that follow. Here is why.

Pet dogs spend most of the time with their people when the folks are home. They use their communication skills letting their family know when to feed them, when to open doors for them, take them for walks (as well as which direction to walk), when to play with them, when to pet them, and sometimes even when to get up in the morning. These are the functions of a leadership role, letting people know how they are supposed to behave, not through a master/slave approach, but through methods that people find pleasant and, therefore, they willingly comply.

However, the time eventually comes when the leader dog, with its feelings of responsibility for the welfare of the pack members, gets abandoned by them, and the dog's subordinates act as if *they* should be directing things. The rules of the game suddenly change and frustration sets in, the contest intensifies, often gets physically rougher, and feelings get hurt on both sides. What might have started out to be an ideal relationship begins to fall apart.

Dogs suffering from what could be called the *Frustrated Leadership Syndrome* behave in ways that relieve their tensions, at least temporarily. These actions are called "Dog Behavior Problems," when in reality they are just symptoms of something else that is going wrong

in daily life. Faced with behavior problems. people often think a training course is the answer, so they send the pet to a school or enroll in obedience classes.

The Need to be Trained

Wild and domestic dogs seem to put a lot of stock in ritual. Wolves ritualize their dominant and subordinate relationships with such displays instead of going through the physical hassle of *proving* things all the time. So do domestic pups.

Obedience classes can be invaluable in this respect, particularly if a puppy has been taught without a leash to follow its owners, come to them when called, sit when asked (and learn not to get up until given permission), and to stay. For a pup given a preschool education, an obedience class is a logical place to learn to get along with life on the end of a leash, especially if puppy classes are available.

Many dogs with serious behavior problems, however, are great performers at obedience work in the local park. Many are also wash-outs. In either case, a simple, daily off-leash ritual in the house in the morning can be extremely helpful. It should be quick and intense, no longer than about three minutes. It needn't involve more than calling the pup or older dog to Come, Sit and Stay (see pages 153-156). Instant praise for each response and a few seconds' affectionate petting when it's finished are all that is required.

What does this accomplish? A few minutes of intense "I'm leading, you're responding" helps to reaffirm the leader-follower relationship. It gives the animal a sense of having functioned and achieved all its leaders' approval, since everybody old enough in the family should conduct the simple exercise. In and of itself I have never seen it correct a behavior problem. As part of a total program, it has been most helpful. The teaching technique is presented in the Puppy section.

The Value of Ritual
One common aspect of obedience-trained problem dogs is that the *ritual* has usually been left at the park or out in the backyard. The Obedience Training and Problems section will go into more detail on the subject.

You can best appreciate the value of ritual in the daily interactions between dogs and their people. One of these is the "Dog nudges, owner pets" routine. You may notice that nearly all the problem corrections take advantage of this ritual. However, they require that the sequence undergo an alteration, as follows: "Dog nudges, owner pleasantly asks for some simple function (such as Sit); dog sits, owner pets."

Some bossy dogs show signs of surprise when asked to *earn* praise and petting. Some even refuse to comply, move away and whine or bark in protest. Others have been known to go away, lie down and sulk, like a pouting child denied a dish of ice cream. However, pouting is effective self-therapy. So in either case, if the behavior is ignored, the dogs soon return and finally get the message that there is a new leader in the group!

FUNDAMENTAL DOG-TALK

Stance and movement speak volumes, compared to the noises dogs make at each other or to people, though each element is important in various situations. A low growl may be a warning to knock off some disturbing activity, or a non-threatening response to an otoscope being stuck in the ear for veterinary inspection.

However, when the growl is heard from a dog standing with tail and hackles raised, the message that a battle could follow is unmistakable.

Besides the usual dominant and submissive postures and movements, dogs develop ways to show submission and happiness by tail-wagging, general excitability, prancing, and even jumping up and down.

FUNDAMENTAL DOG TALK

Dogs show submission and happiness by tail-wagging, excitability, prancing, and jumping up and down.

FUNDAMENTAL DOG TALK

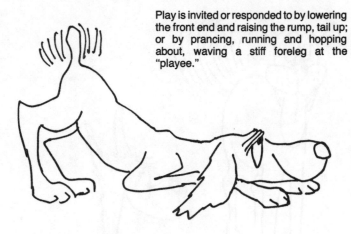

Play is invited or responded to by lowering the front end and raising the rump, tail up; or by prancing, running and hopping about, waving a stiff foreleg at the "playee."

FUNDAMENTAL DOG TALK

A frontal approach, with direct eye contact, tail and ears up, and hackles raised, is a sign that attack or a "bluff" is in the offing.

Circling another animal or person is dominant. Allowing it is somewhat submissive.

FUNDAMENTAL DOG TALK

A paw raised, with bent foreleg, is a submissive, friendly gesture.

FUNDAMENTAL DOG TALK

An absolutely still stance, with tail and ears up and the eyes rolled away, signals a readiness to fight, or that attack may be the next social gesture.

FUNDAMENTAL DOG TALK

A central position in a group can indicate a dog who either feels insecure, or "leader" of the group.

FUNDAMENTAL DOG TALK

Insecure and/or over-protective dogs often "cut out" a stranger by walking or running between them and the family.

FUNDAMENTAL DOG TALK

A playful nip from the rear can mean a friendly "How-dee-do," or a mild form of objection to something that is going on.

FUNDAMENTAL DOG TALK

Taking a hand, arm or leg and holding it in the mouth signals a bossy dog.

Shoulder-bumping a person's leg, especially when they first start to walk somewhere, is the sign of a bossy dog, although some herding breeds do it with no bossy intent.

FUNDAMENTAL DOG TALK

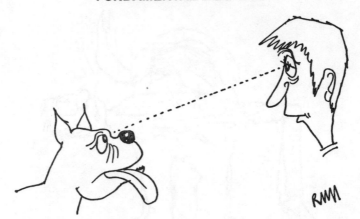

Direct eye contact, with or without expectant tail-wagging, but with no aggressive signs, says, "Pay attention to me!"

A nose "bunt" can signal a friendly greeting. It may also mean "Thank you" after you give water to a thirsty dog.

FUNDAMENTAL DOG TALK

Nudging with the muzzle or nose says "Pet me!"

Bossy dogs often take an outside position in a group, where they can "keep an eye" on everyone.

FUNDAMENTAL DOG TALK

"Come-hither" movements tell us to follow.

FUNDAMENTAL DOG TALK

Some pets show their teeth in a kind of snarling smile, especially when greeting people. (I call this a "snile," or "smarl.") It is usually shown by submissive types, and is often misunderstood as being aggressive.

A paw on the leg is generally a friendly invitation for petting or play, or means "Pay attention and await the next command!"

FUNDAMENTAL DOG TALK

Pet dogs adapt to and learn about human body language, too. If you crouch, especially sidewise toward a puppy or dog, they will usually approach in a friendly manner.

FUNDAMENTAL DOG TALK

When its owners stand or walk side-by-side with outsiders, most dogs interpret this as a friendly relationship.

FUNDAMENTAL DOG TALK

Face-to-face meetings between owners and outsiders may trigger aggression. This may be learned from witnessing family arguments, which are usually conducted from similar positions.

FUNDAMENTAL DOG TALK

When a stranger stands or sits *within* the family group, the dog may interpret it as pack-invasion, even when people are side-by-side.

FUNDAMENTAL DOG TALK

Standing stock still in the presence of an aggressive dog may trigger attack. It is better to stand sideways to the dog, leaning slightly away from it, and turning smoothly with it if it starts to circle. Avoid *locking* into direct eye-contact.

5
The Dog's Problem: People

or

The Great Miscommunicators

Unfortunately, you and I cannot sit down and discuss your dog's behavior problem. If we could, I would be able to spot certain things in your environment that are creating difficulties. Then I could consult in such a way that would allow you to discover the various frustrations in the dog's life. Insight gained through self-discovery usually affects human attitudes and behavior which, in turn, can change a dog's behavior for the better.

However, since we cannot chat about things, the next best approach must be to reveal the main human elements that beget problem-dogs. Among these you may recognize things that relate to your situation. With the background gained from the earlier chapters about dogs, you should then be able to make various adjustments in your environment, select the appropriate correction program, and start on your way to an effective, humane solution.

THE HUMAN ELEMENT

The following profiles of problem-people and environments are deliberately exaggerated for effect, and are not intended to "put down" my clients, upon whom they are based, or your situation. In fact, I recognize myself in most of the profiles, especially the Domineering-Physical-Verbal type. So don't let your feelings be hurt.

91

Name-Droppers

Name-Droppers sit around and talk a lot *about* their dogs, using the pet's name. Then they claim the animal ignores them when they use the same name to talk *to* it, little realizing that they "trained" the nonresponse.

These folks will benefit if they give the dog *two* names; a new one to use for talking *about* it, and the old one, to be used only when speaking *to* the dog. Use of the dog's own name should be followed by praise and petting, before feeding, and in various other situations. Excellent response usually is seen in a day.

Back-Talkers

Back-Talkers usually put the dog's name *after* a command word, *eg,* "Sit, Tippy." When they realize that dogs do not hear backward, they turn things around and begin communicating effectively.

"Sit, Tippy!"

"Down!"

Yo-Yo Makers

Yo-Yo Makers, often children, shout "Down!" while quickly raising their hands up away from the dog, which signals Up. Some dogs learn to do both (Yo-Yo's) while others simply continue to jump.

When Yo-Yo Makers learn to crouch down or reach down to pet the dog before it jumps, most jumping problems are resolved.

Pointers

Pointers stand rigidly upright with a demanding forefinger aimed at a spot by their side or feet, telling the dog to Come. They rarely realize they are actually communicating "Stay still, like I am." Worse yet, they may be sending a message of aggressiveness and/or impending punishment.

Pointers are generally amazed at how quickly their pets learn to Come when they crouch, clap and praise.

Whirling Dervishes

Nearly always late leaving for work, Whirling Dervishes race around the house getting ready, winding up their pet's misbehavioral

The Whirling Dervish

mainspring. Then they suddenly disappear, leaving the dog to un-wind. Setting the alarm clock five minutes earlier than usual and getting up when it goes off can correct the Dervish situation.

Neat-Freaks

Neat-Freaks are usually women, but not always. They must make sure that everything is in its proper place before leaving the house. They walk around adjusting throw-pillows, moving books, etc, while their ever-watchful dog takes careful note. When left alone, the pet continues the chore, finding the owner's fresh scent often too irresistable not to chew on.

The Neat Freak

To solve this problem most Neat-Freaks have to break their own habits, though wearing surgical gloves during the tidying ritual has helped in mild cases.

Domineering-Physical

Domineering-Physical types are "hands-on" people. You see them pushing down on their pet's rump, even when the dog knows the word Sit. They don't praise much, either.

You can identify this type from their person-to-person body language. They tend to crowd people, standing very close, usually face-to-face, with steady, unfaltering eye contact. They also invite people through doors ahead of them, then help them along with a hand on the shoulder or arm.

The Domineering-Physical Type

With their dogs, they are usually Pointers (the human type), or they spank, swat, beat and sometimes kick if the dog misbehaves. This is usually motivated by the old "Me master, You slave" attitude about dogs. Sticking a pet's nose into its urine or feces is popular as a housetraining technique with these types.

Domineering-Physical types are usually men, but can be women and children, especially if they are copying Father.

Domineering-Physical types can become excellent with dogs, once they learn and use successfully the nonphysical approaches. Once enlightened, they often ask, "Does this work with kids, too?"

Domineering-Vocal

The Drill-Sergeant syndrome is found in people with all sorts of personalities. It comes about most often through failure to reinforce the dog's desirable responses with liberal praise and some quick

"Heel! . . . Heel!"

The Drill Sergeant

petting. This stems from believing "Once the dog learns, praise should not be required."

When persons of this type give the pet a second name for talking about it and understand that withholding praise extinguishes responses and can create neurotic dogs, they are usually on their way to patching up their pet relationships.

Seductive-Physical/Vocal

Seductive-Physical/Vocal types attempt to gain the pet's loyalty and obedience through petting of a sensuous nature, usually called "fondling" often accompanied by "sweet talk." Male owners rarely use this approach with male dogs, but often feel it's OK to be seen using it with female pets. Women and children use it with both sexes, since neither evidently suffers from concern about a macho image.

A wise and well-known American psychiatrist has said, in effect, "House-pet owners who do not recognize that there is a sexual element in their animal relationships are just not being honest with themselves."

When the precopulatory facets of *stroking* the dog (or cat) are understood, most Seductive-Physical types reserve petting as a reward for *doing* something desirable.

Seductive-Vocal types often suffer from the "Tippy understands every word I say" condition. Once they appreciate that a sympathetic tone of voice communicates only worried concern to the pet, rather than reassurance, an upbeat or more matter-of-fact tone is usually adopted.

Insecure-Permissive

Insecure-Permissive types want their dog's affection and often lose it by giving in, allowing things like getting up on the furniture, except when guests are present, at which time the pet tries to get up and is scolded or punished. The inconsistency of the relationship frustrates the dog and leads to problems. Depending on the type of dog, the problems range from submissive wetting to outright viciousness toward the owners and/or guests.

Most Insecure-Permissive persons are very pleasant and easy to get along with among people, but often complain privately that others take advantage of their good nature. So do their dogs! Many of them, after seeing the benefits of applying good-natured but consistent guidance with their dogs, have told me they have even started saying "No" to unreasonable requests from their family and friends. As a result, their self-esteem is growing by leaps and bounds.

Ambivalent

Ambivalent types suffer from the classic love-hate relationship. That is, they love the dog, but hate its behavior. Most of them are considering getting rid of the pet, but say that they "want to do everything possible to solve the problem" before making that fateful decision.

I tell Ambivalent types the truth, and it usually lays the foundation for a successful problem correction. The truth is this: Making that fateful decision to keep the dog is the first required step in "doing everything possible to solve the problem."

Problem-dog owners who think they can *act* as if they are committed to a lifelong relationship with a pet, but are thinking about scrapping that relationship, sell short the animal's emotional and observational sensitivities. Dogs can sense insincerity and ambivalence in their owners quicker than they can spot a goodie dropped from the dinner table.

On the other hand, when the firm decision is made to keep the dog, no matter what happens, I have seen serious problems such as household urination clear up in a day!

I'm hoping you have already made your decision in the dog's favor.

"Paranoid" Pet People

I put "Paranoid" in quotes because it is used here in a lighthearted sense. But I have seen pet owners who would swear on the Bible that their dog or cat "has it in for them." Most often the pet is seen as "getting even" or "punishing" the owner.

If spiteful behavior does exist in pets, it must have been learned from people, because all the wild dog-watchers in the world have yet to see it! The solution is to change the supposedly spiteful behavior by removing its cause.

The Logician, or Common-Sense Addict

Common sense leads to such sayings as "What goes up must come down," which fit handily the knowledge of its day. However, new information calls for a closer look at old ideas, since we now know that what goes up may never descend—at least to where it started from.

In the world of dog behavior problems there are all sorts of corrections that appeal to common sense. Most of these concern doing something to the dog. For instance, it makes some sort of sense that if you fill a freshly dug hole in the yard with water and then stuff your canine excavator's head into it until it almost passes out, the dog will avoid digging in the area. As a matter of fact, most dogs actually will avoid digging there again. Even more predictably, however, they find somewhere else in the yard to dig. So instead of the problem being solved, it spreads as the dog continues trying to work off that tension.

Another "logical" solution concerns chewing up pillows and the like. This one says that if you stuff the chewed-up material in the dog's mouth, tape the mouth shut and leave it for some time, the dog will not chew that material anymore. This is sensible if you want your

The Logician's Approach to Chewing

dog to avoid already chewed-up things, such as the remnants of pillows. However, a little more common sense might bring one to the conclusion that unchewed pillows is what the dog ought to avoid.

In the meantime, applying these seemingly logical techniques tears at the fabric of an already stressed relationship. Frustration mounts, anxieties and tensions become stronger, and problems get worse. Too often the Logican concludes there is something abnormal about the pet, and gets rid of it.

Let's hope this logic convinces more and more common-sense types that there is a better way.

Naive First-Timers and "Model"-Buyers

Naive types have never owned a pet before and usually select one that fits their preformed ideas about how a dog or cat ought to behave. When the animal doesn't fit the notion, naive types usually follow everybody's advice, at least for a day or two. They are great book-buyers, too. Let's hope this one helps!

"Experimenters" are usually recently married and want to use the pet (generally a dog) as a test animal on which to practice parenting (first-child syndrome). The trouble with this is that puppies mature to the juvenile level so quickly that the "parents" usually cannot make adjustments in their areas of disagreement before serious problems occur. The best advice for these naive types is to raise dogs and cats as pets and raise children as children.

Model-Buyers are not necessarily naive, but they obtain dogs with the misconception that certain breeds always behave in certain ways. This myth is roundly supported and propagated by most dog breeders and the media, especially movies. When the behavior doesn't fit the myth, some model-buyers go back to the breeders for a trade-in. Some breeders actually take trade-ins.

If you are a disappointed model-buyer, I hope the first four chapters have helped you understand your pet's unique development and its dependence on you.

The Jekyll & Hyde Syndrome

We all have our ups and downs, but sufferers of the Jekyll and Hyde Syndrome show them to their dogs with gusto. They leave their problem dog in the morning with apologies and words of consolation usually based on feelings of guilt. All this convinces the dog that there really is something *wrong* with being alone, so it gets anxious and tense. Then, off to work goes kindly Dr. Jekyll.

When he returns home and finds that the dog has misbehaved, the diabolical Mr. (or Mrs.) Hyde roars into action. Ranting, raving, scolding and/or punishment now convince the pet that homecomings are also something to worry about. Thereafter, the specter of Mr. Hyde's arrival creates enough anxiety for some more tension-relieving misbehavior.

Jekyll and Hyde types usually change their behavior when they understand facts about the dog's biological clock, its inability to associate previous misbehavior with delayed punishment, and the need for consistency in human behavior to provide the reliable leadership dogs need.

Problem Children

Most kids get along well with dogs when the parents provide gentle and enlightened guidance to both. However, when emotional and/or physical parental excesses take place, children and dogs both tend to react according to the "Be-like, Act-like" principle mentioned earlier.

For instance, if you get angry and scold or punish a child a lot, your dog may start getting edgy when the youngster is around it. On the other hand, if you do the same to your dog, the child may start playing your role and get into trouble when the pet defends itself.

I am not in the child-parent consultation profession, but I have seen enough pet misbehavior as a result of troubles in that area to offer one piece of advice: If you have family problems, seek some competent guidance about them while you work on your pet's problems as well.

With that said, there are still some things children do with dogs that can be the basis for both mild and serious problems. The following table lists them. Be sure to keep the "Be-like, Act-like" principle in mind in handling them.

Dr. Jekyll

"Bye, Bruno, poor lonesome boy! Be good, Bruno baby! Daddy see you tonight!"

Mr. Hyde

"So! You've been bad again! Bruno!"

Children's Roles in Dog Behavior Problems

Child Behavior	Dog Response
Pulling ears, tail, hair; sticking fingers in ears, eyes	Growling, snapping, biting
Hitting with hands or objects	Growling, snapping, biting, submissive wetting in pups
Teasing with toys, food; staring, wrestling to the point of anger or rage	Biting, viciousness
Encouraging aggressiveness toward outsiders, other dogs, cats, birds, etc.	Biting, viciousness, chasing, dog-fighting, cat-killing, bird-killing, escaping, barking
Tidbitting with food	Begging, overprotectiveness of food, food-stealing
Playing tug-of-war	Biting, stealing things, chewing
Screaming and/or running	Biting, jumping, chasing
Scolding, punishing	Growling, biting
Being unruly	Being unruly
Interchild fighting	Aggressiveness, biting, over-excitability
Sexual stimulation, especially of male dogs	Mounting, aggressiveness, urinating in house, biting other children

My Dog-Your Dog Jealousy

A young married couple had a chewing two-year-old spayed Doberman. I always ask clients why they selected a certain breed of dog. The answer in this case was protection, which in these times is not unreasonable. The next question is why they got the sex they did.

She answered, "Oh, Bob picked her, probably because he knew that females like men better than women."

Bob's rejoinder was immediate: "Not at all, Martha. I didn't get a male because I was sure you'd spoil him so much that he'd get overprotective of you!"

"Well," Martha retorted, "she's your dog and it's your problem. I just came along because Bill said it would be helpful."

If looks could kill, Bob would have been on his way to the mortuary. Meanwhile the dog began to whine.

I broke the mood, saying, "Since you've put your finger on the problem, let's figure out how to resolve it."

With that, we were on our way to working with the "Green-Monster Syndrome," which is often involved in all sorts of problems. Jealousy over a dog is tough to work out, since it is usually never expressed openly. Bob and Martha were exceptions to the rule.

If you think this might be an element in your situation, take hope. There is a way to bring the monster out of hiding and slay it: Talk about it. But, if you think things are going to get emotionally hot, spare the dog. Go out to dinner or take a walk. Discuss your hangups and agree on how you are going to conduct whatever correction program fits your problem. Then, as the preacher may have said after your marriage ceremony, "Good luck!"

PROBLEM ENVIRONMENTS

War Zones

War Zones are households with two or more people and one or more dogs. The people spend a goodly amount of time firing verbal blasts at one another. These are low-level holding actions, or they can be

full-scale attacks. They are sometimes accompanied by hand-to-hand combat, especially if teenage children live there.

Not all War Zones are so evident. Some involve intermittent sniping, which takes the form of verbal zingers, usually aimed at the ego-structure of the enemy.

In either case, the problem-dog gets into the action one way or another: directly by joining the combat forces through aggressiveness or barking, or indirectly in ways ranging from chewing to self-mutilation.

War Zones often require professional mediation, but at least warrant a stable truce if the dog's problem is going to be solved.

Hermitages

Hermitages are at the opposite extreme from War Zones. Usually occupied by one person and one dog, they can also have several of each. The people don't like outsiders, so the pup never, never gets to find out about them, except for trips to the veterinarian. In extreme cases, housecall veterinarians are used.

Under such conditions, active, socially outgoing dogs can develop problems ranging from unruliness to aggressiveness. Calm, submissive-types usually do better.

The Fortress Syndrome

The Fortress Syndrome is seen in households where people distrust nearly everyone. Windows are peeked out of when cars pass or pull up. Every noise is investigated to see if prowlers might be in the yard, or out in the hall, if the fortress is an apartment.

"Well, you got the dog to protect you against criminals. Perhaps now you'll have to hire a criminal to protect you from the dog."

Fortresses are often established as a reasonable response to burglaries or as a result of residing in a high-crime area. Dogs residing in fortresses can acquire problems of all sorts, but usually bark too much or become overaggressive.

PS: If I left you or some other problem-people type out, drop me a line with a full description and we'll see about putting it in the next edition.

6

The Puppy Primer

or

How to Avoid Creating a Problem Dog

If you are looking for a puppy or just got one, this chapter is dedicated to that cherished little ball of fur and fun, with a fond wish for good luck!

If you haven't read the first five chapters yet, save yourself some time and do so—very carefully. Much of the advice here runs counter to the traditional way of bringing a pup into a human household, and knowing the reasons behind it will help you and your new puppy benefit from easier and better ways to raise a canine companion.

WHY A DOG?

If you haven't had a discussion among all those who are going to live with the future pet, have one. This can bring up all sorts of sources for human conflict about the dog *before* you get it, especially in families with children.

For instance, many a pup has wound up in the laundry room on its first night because the children got into a fight over whose bedroom it would sleep in. The "Why A Dog" discussion can help gain agreement from everyone on the most important issues in puppy-raising. These are:

- Where will the puppy sleep at night
- Where will it be kept in the daytime
- What housetraining method will be used
- Who will feed the puppy
- Who will clean up the pup's messes

- Who will take the puppy out for toilet and socializing
- How will the puppy be taught commands and who will do the teaching
- If the pup is to be scolded or punished, who will do it and for what reasons
- Who will bathe, brush and groom the pup
- What kind of play will be taught
- Will it be allowed on furniture
- Will it be given food tidbits

These are elements that create family friction and can lead to serious behavior problems if people do not agree and consistently live up to their agreements. It's better to debate them before the puppy arrives than introduce it into a "war zone."

WHAT TYPE OF DOG?

Big, medium or small; skinny, heavy or medium body type; long, medium or short coat? No matter the breed, these are things that need consideration from a behavioral standpoint.

Here is a list of physical traits that have been the basis for problems, due to human conflicts about them.

"Some people think they're ugly. I think they're appealing!"

Picking your breed may be easy!

Hair, or Coat Types

Short hair: The reason it's short is not because it doesn't grow; these dogs shed, all the time. The hair works its way into carpets and upholstery and is extremely hard to extract therefrom.

Medium length, straight hair: These dogs also shed, and many have undercoats that come out in great gobs at regular intervals.

Curly hair, medium and long: These dogs require regular grooming, but some do not shed. Instead, they pick up fox-tails, dirt and debris and shed these around the house. They also may come into the house with bits of feces hanging from their rumps.

Tail and Nose Types

Long tails: They can clear off coffee and end tables. They can hurt when making contact with persons while in full-wag.

Pug-nosed types: Some of them snort a lot, and sometimes their noses emit a spray.

Loose-lipped types: Some of them drool uncontrollably.

These are the physical traits that have created problems, not by themselves but by their effect on the people living with the pets. It is a pity that any dog would find itself banished to the backyard for life, or hustled away from visitors because of its physical characteristics. However, it does happen, and can lead to problems.

Size of Dog

Giant Size: They usually get much bigger than people expect. Problems can crop up in cars, and in walking on leashes. Visitors are sometimes frightened of them.

Large Size: See Giant Size.

Miniature Size: They are sometimes underfoot when you least expect them. Also, people tend to pick them up a good deal.

Toy Size, Teacup Size: See Miniature Size.

When you have selected your type and breed of dog, make sure everyone has considered the possible negative social reactions they may feel about any of these traits.

SELECTING A PUPPY

A simple test can help you decide, from among all those cuddly balls of fur, which pup would be best suited to you and your environment.

The idea for the test came to me after so many of my clients said, "I wish you could have seen him in the litter. He was so cute. Who would have thought he'd be such a problem?"

As a matter of fact, I would have! Pups have certain tendencies that begin to emerge as they pass about three-and-one-half weeks of age. These tendencies, such as dominance, submissiveness and independence, will be revealed by my test. Once you know them, your decision for *the* puppy can be made with more insight.

PUPPY BEHAVIOR TEST

The first step is to gain the breeder's agreement to the test. Once advised that it is merely a handling procedure, most breeders are delighted that you are going to make special efforts to select the right pup. The best age for testing is between five and seven weeks, but up to twelve weeks is still all right. Assign each pup a letter, to correspond with the score sheet.

When you first see the litter, observe from a distance and try to pick out who is most bossy, most shy, playful, etc. You may be surprised to note how differently they behave when you get them away and alone with you.

With the breeder, select an area about 20 by 20 feet out of sight and earshot of the litter. There must not be any distraction stronger than you in the area.

Social Attraction and Following

Pick up the first puppy from the litter and go to the test area. Walk to the center of the area, put the pup down facing you and walk away, looking back at it as you go. Then crouch down facing the pup and gently clap your hands to attract it to you.

If the pup follows or comes readily, tail up, perhaps jumps on you and even bites at your hands, score it dd, double dominant.

If it comes readily with tail up, but does not bite or jump boldly, score it d.

If it comes, tail not up and sidles a bit as it nears, score a single s for submissive.

If it approaches with extreme shyness, perhaps even rolling over or urinating, give an ss for super-submissive.

This procedure should take about 30 seconds. When finished, stand up and start walking away from the pup. Even if you have to walk in circles, keep walking until the puppy either follows or does not follow.

If it does not follow, score an i for independent.

If it follows and tries to impede your progress and even bites at your feet, score a dd. If it follows, tail up, but does not bite or try to impede progress, give it a d.

If it follows, tail not up, with no attempt to impede you, score an s. If it lags or does not follow, but seems to want to, score an ss.

Restraint Dominance

Restraint Dominance is next. Gently roll the puppy onto its back, holding it with only one hand by the chest. Place your thumb and little finger under the pup's armpits to stabilize it. Hold firmly, without causing pain, for 30 seconds.

If the pup fights wildly all the time, even bites at your hand, score a dd. If it fights, but is not wild, score a d.

If it fights, but only for a few seconds and then settles, score an s. If it does not fight at all, give it an ss.

PUPPY BEHAVIOR TEST

BEHAVIOR CATEGORIES

SOCIAL ATTRACTION — Select one:

1. Came readily-tail up-jumped-bit at hands
2. Came readily-tail up-pawed at hands
3. Came readily-tail down
4. Came, hesitant-tail down
5. Did not come at all

FOLLOWING — Select one:

1. Followed readily-tail up-bit at feet
2. Followed readily-tail up-got underfoot
3. Followed readily-tail down
4. Followed, hesitant-tail down
5. No follow or went away

RESTRAINT DOMINANCE (30 sec.) Select one:

1. Struggled fiercely-flailed-bit
2. Struggled fiercely-flailed
3. Struggled, then settled
4. No struggle-licked at hands

SOCIAL DOMINANCE (30 sec.) Select one:

1. Jumped-pawed-bit-growled
2. Jumped-pawed
3. Squirmed-licked at hands
4. Rolled over-licked at hands
5. Went and stayed away

ELEVATION DOMINANCE (30 sec.) Select one:

1. Struggled fiercely-bit-growled
2. Struggled fiercely
3. Struggled-settled-licked
4. No struggle-licked at hands

Assign each pup a letter (A, B, C, etc.). Circle the code letters scored under each pup's letter in each test section.

PUPS:	A	B	C	D	E	F	G	H	I	J	K	L	M	N	O	P
SOCIAL ATTRACTION																
1.	dd	dd	dd	dd	dd	dd	dd	dd	dd	dd	dd	dd	dd	dd	dd	dd
2.	d	d	d	d	d	d	d	d	d	d	d	d	d	d	d	d
3.	s	s	s	s	s	s	s	s	s	s	s	s	s	s	s	s
4.	ss	ss	ss	ss	ss	ss	ss	ss	ss	ss	ss	ss	ss	ss	ss	ss
5.	i	i	i	i	i	i	i	i	i	i	i	i	i	i	i	i
FOLLOWING																
1.	dd	dd	dd	dd	dd	dd	dd	dd	dd	dd	dd	dd	dd	dd	dd	dd
2.	d	d	d	d	d	d	d	d	d	d	d	d	d	d	d	d
3.	s	s	s	s	s	s	s	s	s	s	s	s	s	s	s	s
4.	ss	ss	ss	ss	ss	ss	ss	ss	ss	ss	ss	ss	ss	ss	ss	ss
5.	i	i	i	i	i	i	i	i	i	i	i	i	i	i	i	i
RESTRAINT DOMINANCE																
1.	dd	dd	dd	dd	dd	dd	dd	dd	dd	dd	dd	dd	dd	dd	dd	dd
2.	d	d	d	d	d	d	d	d	d	d	d	d	d	d	d	d
3.	s	s	s	s	s	s	s	s	s	s	s	s	s	s	s	s
4.	ss	ss	ss	ss	ss	ss	ss	ss	ss	ss	ss	ss	ss	ss	ss	ss
SOCIAL DOMINANCE																
1.	dd	dd	dd	dd	dd	dd	dd	dd	dd	dd	dd	dd	dd	dd	dd	dd
2.	d	d	d	d	d	d	d	d	d	d	d	d	d	d	d	d
3.	s	s	s	s	s	s	s	s	s	s	s	s	s	s	s	s
4.	ss	ss	ss	ss	ss	ss	ss	ss	ss	ss	ss	ss	ss	ss	ss	ss
5.	i	i	i	i	i	i	i	i	i	i	i	i	i	i	i	i
ELEVATION DOMINANCE																
1.	dd	dd	dd	dd	dd	dd	dd	dd	dd	dd	dd	dd	dd	dd	dd	dd
2.	d	d	d	d	d	d	d	d	d	d	d	d	d	d	d	d
3.	s	s	s	s	s	s	s	s	s	s	s	s	s	s	s	s
4.	ss	ss	ss	ss	ss	ss	ss	ss	ss	ss	ss	ss	ss	ss	ss	ss

TOTALS:

	A	B	C	D	E	F	G	H	I	J	K	L	M	N	O	P
dd's =																
d's =																
s's =																
ss's =																
i's =																

Social Dominance

Now sit the pup in front of you for the Social Dominance section. Pet it gently on the back of its neck and shoulders.

If it bites at your hands or growls score a dd. If it merely seems to object, score it a d.

If it seems to enjoy the petting, whether or not it turns its head, score an s. If it licks at your hands, perhaps even rolls over, score an ss.

Elevation Dominance

Elevation Dominance is the final test. Make a cradle of your hands under the pup's chest by interlacing your fingers. Lift up the pup so it is balanced in your hands off the floor or ground by about five inches. Hold it there for 30 seconds.

If it struggles fiercely, bites or growls, score a dd. If it merely struggles all the time, score a d.

If it struggles but settles, score an s. If no struggle at all occurs, score an ss.

MAKING YOUR SELECTION

What the scores indicate:

Two dd's with other d's indicate the pup may not be well suited for infants or older folks and may be difficult to handle. If selected, take it through this test daily until it accepts dominant handling.

Three or more d's, even with a dd, indicate an outgoing, bossy pup. Rough physical handling should be avoided. Conducting this test daily can be beneficial.

Three or more s's indicate a pup that usually fits well in most situations.

Two or more ss's indicate a pup who may be highly submissive, needing lots of praise and gentle handling. Heavy-handedness can ruin this type of puppy.

As you conduct the test and compute the scores, here are some things to keep in mind:

• You are making the preliminary test, but if you still have doubts, have other family members test the puppies also. This gets everyone involved, and you may find some pups who react differently, especially to children.

• Puppies who test (i), for independent, in the Attraction, Following, and Dominance sections are not necessarily "bad" as pets. If they are selected, they will tend more than others to be a one-person dog. Even then, especially if they test (dd) in the dominance sections, they will require regular daily exercise of the test sections, or it may be difficult for you to gain a leading, dominant position.

• When conducting the test, it is best to have an observer who can see into the area without being apparent to the puppy. Let this person keep the scores. This way, you can run the sequence smoothly, without having to stop and make notes.

Whichever puppy you select, remember that it will change as it matures within your own environment. Extensive testing of puppies that have been selected with this test indicates that between about four and seven months of age the pup may seem to belie its "type." However, as it matures further, it will tend to revert to type. Your greatest advantage in using the test is that you make the final decision after handling each puppy on a one-to-one basis.

With your choice made, it's time for the ride home.

The Ride Home

Riding home in the car may be the puppy's first experience with mechanical monsters, so it's important that it be as pleasant as you can make it. Put the pup on a towel or blanket, beside someone or on a lap. If the weather is cold, warm up the car; if hot, cool it down, if possible. Cold or heat stress can help create a lifelong carsickness tendency, so try to avoid it.

If the pup vomits, urinates or defecates, don't fuss. Just clean it up and carry on.

Some puppies naturally start whining, yelping or wailing. Don't try to punish it out of the little one. Just put a reassuring hand on it and continue homeward.

The Arrival

When you get home, put Mother Nature to work right away on the housetraining program. Take the pup immediately to the spot for its future toilet area. When it performs, do the point-and-praise routine and hope the puppy sniffs its deposit and the general area. If not, just take it into the house so it gets the basic impression that going inside follows performance of its outdoor duties.

When you get inside, let the puppy investigate. If everyone sits around in a circle on the floor it will give the pup a chance to get to know and identify everyone by smell, since it can't see too well yet. Let everyone interact naturally with the new pet. This is no time to be "walking on eggs" or for criticism of the way anyone is behaving. However, if someone gets nipped too hard, have them roll the nipper over into the Restraint Dominance position (page 115) and hold it there until it calms down. Then, release it with praise and pet it according to the Social Dominance routine (page 118).

Have fun until the puppy gets tired, then show it the bed. A blanket in an upturned cardboard carton in which you have cut a doorway has many advantages. It affords the puppy its own place where people can't accidentally drop something or step on it, and most pups enjoy getting into something at sleeping time. This arrangement is also portable, so it can be easily carried from one room to another the first night.

Housetraining
If you follow the Housetraining program (page 141) strictly, you will be amazed at how quickly you have a fastidious puppy. Read it until you can almost recite it, so you don't miss any of the steps, especially with regard to the two important phases involved.

The First Night

You can find all sorts of advice on how to isolate your puppy on the first night in a new home. I will not comment on these, except to say that if you intend to stick your new pet away somewhere alone, brace yourself! Steel yourself against doing *anything* in response to the racket you'll have to endure.

Your puppy probably slept through the night quietly among its littermates the night before, so I have found the best plan is to take the sleeping box into someone's bedroom. Put it right next to the bed, where the puppy can hear the breathing sounds of another living being. Most pups will sleep nicely in this situation, at least until a reasonable hour the next morning, when another opportunity for housetraining occurs.

Socializing

From the time you get a puppy until it is several months old it needs exposure to and guidance in all the situations you think it will face in life. This includes happy trips in the car to various places, including the veterinarian. Use the Jolly Routine before, during and after trips to the clinic or hospital. Show it around to all the personnel who may have to handle it one day. This will make everybody happy. Gaining an early, friendly impression with patients forms the basis for a peaceful future relationship for all.

Three trips a week out into the big, wide world will help round out a balanced personality in your dog. These might include visits to airports, the countryside, schools and the like, with opportunities for meeting children, old folks, and other animals. (Ask the doctor about health restrictions that might be necessary.)

Just as going out is important, so is having people into the house to meet the puppy. Make special efforts in this area and you will be able to mold a socially delightful canine companion for life.

These are the vital points involved in selecting and bringing a puppy into the human fold so as to avoid behavior problems. If you already have another dog, or are having a new baby soon, consult the program on "Babies, New Pets and Dogs." If that old puppy bug-a-boo Chewing is on your mind, consult that program. When you have digested these first six chapters, you should be on your way to a rewarding future.

It is a good idea to pick up a puppy a couple of times a day, especially the larger breeds.

7
Adopting an Older Dog

Before you finally adopt an older dog, everyone in the household must agree that you are getting the dog to *keep* it. If you try to adopt an older dog with the idea that you will "see how it goes," one or more behavior problems are likely to arise. This is because the dog has already lost at least one "family" and will arrive with feelings of social insecurity. When you couple these feelings with its ability to *sense* whether or not it is wholeheartedly accepted as part of its new group, you can appreciate that the animal could suffer a double dose of insecurity.

Also, you can expect that the dog probably had some behavior problem in its former home, even though most people who abandon dogs or take them to humane societies or pounds do not like to reveal these problems. This is to be expected. After all, they want the dog to be placed in a nice home, so telling about "Jake the Ripper" or "Chi-Chi the Chewer" is contrary to their and the dog's interests.

However, even if the dog had a behavior problem in its last home, it needn't carry it over to yours if you follow this adoption program. It is based on experience from adopting more than 100 genuine "problem dogs." These pets came with problems ranging from viciousness and fighting to incurable housesoiling. Within four days, most of them settled in as if they had arrived as puppies, and the problems either did not erupt in our home or were cleared up through the correction programs contained here.

Adoption Program

Commitment

As mentioned above, commitment by all members is vital to success.

Selecting the Dog

Always try to select the dog at the home or facility offering it rather than at your home. This avoids stress on the dog, since, if you decide against adopting the dog, it can become more confused than it already is.

Take the whole family along, including any other pets, if possible. If you already have a dog(s), make sure you have read the program for Babies, New Pets and Dogs and follow the instructions, even in the neutral area off their home property.

Once you have made your preliminary selection, find out all you can about the dog's health and behavioral history. If these don't reveal anything objectionable, make sure of everyone's commitment and you are ready for the trip home.

The Ride Home

The only rule here is not to "fuss" over the dog. Let it settle down in its own time in the section of the vehicle where it will travel in the future, whether that is in the back or front seat. Expect the dog to be a little "hyper" at first, but don't try to pet or soothe this out of the animal, as it may think you are approving of its behavior and anxiety.

Arriving at Home

Just as with a puppy, arrival at the new home is a great time to teach an older dog its new toilet area. Take the dog into the house, give it some water and immediately take it out to the place you want it to use as a toilet area. Stand there neutrally, let it investigate. When it urinates or defecates, point at its urine or feces and say, "Good Dog." Pet the dog happily and head back for the house.

The Need To Investigate

When you get everyone in the house again, let the dog go about the place sniffing and checking out things. Do not follow it, otherwise it can get the idea that it is *leader* of its new pack, so to speak. Go about your normal family business.

Sniffing and checking things out

The Search for Leadership

One of the first things the new dog will look for after satisfying its curiosity about the physical environment is leadership, or "Who calls the shots around here?" Depending on its experience with its former owners, it can behave in so many different ways that your only safe course is to apply the principles of leadership.

The first rule of establishing leadership is to ask the dog to do something to gain praise. When it seeks your attention and approval, calmly say, "Tippy, sit." Most older dogs already know the "sit" command, so compliance is quickly obtained. Then praise and pet the dog briefly and continue whatever you were doing.

If the dog keeps pestering you for attention, it gives you a good chance to find out the extent of its learned commands. Ask it to "sit," praise and pet it, and then tell it, "Tippy, down," as you slowly bring your hand, palm up, down through its visual field to a spot in front of its feet on the floor. You'd be amazed how many such commands can be taught a "new" older dog when it is first in its new home, and highly motivated to please. Keep the learn-to-earn routine going as a part of daily life for at least six weeks.

Feeding

If possible, have some of the dog's previously fed food on hand. This avoids the digestive upsets and "accidents" that can arise from abrupt diet changes. Feed the new dog twice a day. This keeps something on its stomach most of the time and avoids *hunger tension* and the problems this can produce.

Sleeping

Dogs should sleep in a room with another living being, rather than isolated. The behavioral tendency to "be like" others around it usually leads to a good night's rest for all.

Most adopted dogs are a bit restless during the first night in their new home. The best reassurance you can provide is to call it back to its sleeping place, praise it and give an affectionate pat, turn out the light and go to sleep.

If your situation dictates that the dog is to sleep alone for the rest of its life, prepare yourself for problems and follow whichever correction program herein fits the predicament that such social isolation produces.

Housetraining

Follow the housetraining program just as if you were dealing with a puppy. Most older dogs respond in a couple of days, if not immediately.

Exercise

Avoid taking your new dog for walks before about six weeks have passed and it has settled in for a permanent stay. Toss a ball or toy for 10-15 minutes a day and it will get plenty of activity. Play is best in the morning, as this tires the animal somewhat and will likely necessitate sleeping during the day if you must leave it alone.

Health Hints

Be sure to take your new dog to a veterinarian for a complete physical examination as soon after you pick it up as possible. No matter what you may have been told about its health history, it is wise to get a check-up. This also allows your veterinarian to become acquainted with the dog and establish a health profile on it in the event of the need for emergency care later.

8
Finding a Lost Dog or Cat

Most owners panic when they cannot locate their pet. However, with a few methodical steps, you can usually find a wanderer or runaway in a matter of hours. The only exceptions are, sadly, when someone finds your pet and is determined to keep it, or when the animal has been killed. The following plan is based on the experiences of many people I have known over the years, as well as my own.

In the 1950's I owned what I did not then know was a hyperkinetic Spaniel mix. This chapter is dedicated to his memory, since he put me through no less than 20 episodes, as he answered his inner "call of the wild." The 21st caper was never solved, as he frantically bayed his way after a herd of elk in the Idaho wilderness. Despite 20 days of searching over a two-month period, we could not locate him. He must have caught up with the elk in deep cover somewhere. Ami, this one's for you.

THE PLAN

Try to determine the time, as closely as possible, when the animal left. Then, even if you have to call the weather bureau, determine the direction of the prevailing wind at that time. Most dogs proceed into the wind, unless they have a favorite direction of running away, in which case you should make that place your first target.

If the escape was within half an hour, you can go upwind or to the favorite place initially. However, if several hours have passed since the animal left, call the local pound and humane authorities with a

description. You may find the animal has already been found. It is also helpful to notify the police, local ambulance and taxi companies, leaving the description and your phone number, plus a friend's number in the event somebody calls while you are out searching.

If there is no wind, it is often best to start your search in the direction the animal observes family members leave your home, or in the direction it travels with you in the car on a regular basis.

Take a picture of the pet with you, even if it is not a recent photograph. Show it to everyone with whom you speak and give them your phone numbers. Canvass your neighborhood thoroughly.

Investigate the following types of places very carefully:

- *Grocery stores, restaurants and anywhere else food is available.* Dogs are often found happily munching on garbage behind such places!
- *Parks, schoolyards and other places that children frequent.* Even check the area around the local zoo.
- *Houses and neighborhoods where you see other dogs or cats, in yards or loose.* Canvass these areas with your photo, even if they are miles from your home.

Get your photo to a quick-copy house and print 100 copies of an 8½ by 11-inch poster, with ½-inch-high letters, as follows:

REWARD
Lost (Date & Time)
Pet's Name
(Photo)
(Pet's name) was last seen at (address). This animal requires a special diet and medical care. If seen or found, please contact (your name) at (phone numbers).

Distribute copies of your poster to schools, playgrounds, parks, fast-food places, markets, restaurants, zoos, pounds, humane societies, veterinary clinics, police stations, taxi companies, ambulance and fire companies, TV and radio stations, churches and all other places with bulletin boards. Do not confine distribution to a single area. Place your posters in all such places within a 5-mile radius from the place of escape.

Place an ad in the classified sections of your newspapers, especially local shopping news publications.

If you suspect the dog or cat may have been taken into a car with someone, widen your search and area of advertising, even to towns within 20 miles of yours.

Keep your posters "fresh." That is, if they get wet or tattered, replace them.

Don't give up. Keep searching for at least 6 months before resigning yourself to the fact that you dog or cat is, indeed, gone from your life.

If this plan does not regain your pet, you may rest assured you have done your utmost.

"Look at the TV, Major! Go get him, boy!"

9
Obedience Training

A Family Affair

Everyone ought to go to an enlightened dog obedience class. Puppy classes can be particularly enriching, but check with your veterinarian regarding possible health restrictions. Please note, I said "everyone" ought to go, meaning the whole family. In this way, your dog will quickly learn to respond to all its people uniformly.

More and more obedience instructors are abandoning the old "one-dog, one-trainer" concept, which was based on the idea that learning from more than a single individual confuses the animal. As a matter of fact, the one-trainer practice can lead to what I call the Beta-dog syndrome, wherein the dog accepts directions and reprimands only from the trainer and feels dominant toward the rest of the family. A bossy, leader-type dog can even start bullying its human underlings.

So a class that encourages full family participation can help you avoid problems.

First Things Third

In obedience class, Come is not taught first. This is probably because you and your pet attend class at opposite ends of a six-foot leash. This avoids the confusion of dogs running loose, and fits the preconception that the attendees are there because they cannot control their animals without a leash.

The result is that Come is taught after Sit and Stay. Further, the initial command to Come is usually taught with the dog and you

131

facing each other, which will be the format of the class graduation test but is not the usual real-world situation, where the command is usually shouted while the dog's attention is focused anywhere but on you.

One way to cope with this situation is to teach the idea of Come using a different word. This is a good practice whether or not you go to obedience class, because it is easy to wear out the power of a panic-command to Come by using it in casual situations. If your dog already will Come despite strong distractions, most obedience instructors allow another word for class exercises.

In nonpanic circumstances, such as around the house, the dog's name followed by praise should bring the desired response if your relationship is a positive one. If not, it's time to look for the reasons and put them right before starting any training.

Nonleash methods for teaching Come, Sit and Stay are in the Puppy Training section. Also, a method for pretraining your dog to walk peacefully with you on the leash is in the Leash-training section. If you and all the family lay a little groundwork, obedience class can be a delightful experience, even with an extremely excitable dog.

Be sure you attend a class where the trainer trains *you*. Before enrolling, ask whether or not the practices of "hanging" or "around the world" are ever used with aggressive dogs. If the answer is yes, your best bet is to find another instructor with more humane methods. The same advice holds true for shock collar devices, no matter what fancy names they may be given.

10

Selecting a
Behavior Consultant

Sometimes an animal's behavior problems seem so involved that they defy our ability to see them objectively, which is when the services of a behavior consultant can be invaluable. The following guide will help ensure that you select someone who will work with you in a way that allows you to gain the insight needed to correct the problem. The little extra time required is well worth spending, compared to the risks of choosing someone based on the size of their Yellow Pages ad or the appeal of their titles.

SELECTING A PET BEHAVIOR SPECIALIST

Have Your Pet Examined

Take your problem-pet to your veterinarian for a complete physical examination. Take along a fresh stool sample for a parasite check. My records of more than 2,000 cases show that more than 20% of dogs with behavior problems who had not been checked in more than 6 months also had a health problem. There is no use wasting money on a behavior problem when there may be a contributing health factor.

Get At Least Two Referrals

After the physical examination, ask the doctor about the behavior problem and whether you might benefit from professional consultation. If the answer is "yes" and a consultant is recommended, ask

what sort of feedback has been received from other clients so referred. Make notes about each specialist.

If any of those clients are acquaintances of yours, talk to them before telephoning any specialists on the list.

Many veterinarians themselves are getting involved in consulting about problems, so if your pet's doctor has some ideas, listen to them. If they sound reasonable and appealing, you might be well advised to follow the veterinarian's suggestions before contacting anyone else. But, give the advice *time* to work and follow the instructions carefully.

Qualifying the Consultants

The telephone call to the specialist is aimed at gathering vital information about how he or she goes about working with owners and their problem pets. But keep in mind, just as you are qualifying them, they are also qualifying you!

If they are operating on the highest ethical standards, they will want to know a great deal about you, your pet and its health history, plus the history of the problem from the beginning to the present time. They should be especially interested in what steps you may have already taken to solve the problem yourself or with other assistance.

Give them all the facts. This will allow them to decide if they can really help, or if they should refer you to someone more specialized in the problem.

On the other hand, if they show no interest in the history of the problem and simply press you for an appointment, count your blessings, thank them nicely, hang up and contact the next consultant on the list. Anyone in this profession who does not extend the courtesy of qualifying his or her clients through a few minutes on the telephone falls into one or more of the following categories:

- They lack the necessary experience and/or training to do it. Why pay them to educate themselves on your animal?
- They subscribe to the new-car dealer's "system house" approach, which states: "You can't get their check and close a deal on the phone." This is not very professional.
- They are too acutely dog- or cat-oriented to appreciate your role in the problem, especially if they use the old story that they must "see" your pet before anything can be decided.
- They are too far up in some academic or scientific Ivory Tower to feel a genuine "empathy" with you as the owner of a problem pet.

Any of the above types display a lack of understanding about the emotional state of someone sincerely seeking help for a pet. They fail to respond as a well-trained consultant should respond, which is with empathy. Add this to the fact that they do not qualify their clients in order to save time, effort and money for all concerned.

Get the Facts and Understand Them

If the specialist offers a description of the programs available, listen carefully and make notes. Be sure all of the following questions are answered to your satisfaction. While you are gathering this information, don't hesitate to interrupt to ask for an explanation of any term or procedure you do not understand. Unfortunately, many competently trained and well-educated behavior specialists tend to use jargon and such terms as "bonding" and "separation anxiety." These are fine for professional seminars but tend to confuse pet owners.

Questions To Ask
- *Where and how long will the appointments be?* 60-90 minutes is usual for appointments.

- *Who must attend?* Make sure everyone involved in the problem and correction procedures can attend.
- *What will we be doing?* Get "operational descriptions," such as sitting and talking, training the dog, etc.
- *How many appointments will be required?* Six weekly meetings usually suffice, even for severe problems.
- *Will any special equipment be required? If so, what?* This will reveal whether or not shock collars, spike collars, hanging nooses, hobbles, ultrasonic devices, etc. will be used. If so, get descriptions of how they will be used.
- *What is the most severe physical treatment that may be required?* This lets you know if ear-biting, kneeing, kicking, hitting, jerking or shaking are part of the program.
- *If the problem persists after the program is completed, what happens?* This will prepare you for further meetings and/or charges if things do not go as expected.
- *How much will it cost?*

With these questions answered, you can qualify the specialist on three accounts:

1. The humaneness of the methods to be employed, which is up to your own, personal tastes.
2. The cost of the program in terms of the money, time and effort you will be investing.
3. What sort of rapport you and the specialist establish. If you and the consultant cannot communicate smoothly during an explanation of the programs, you're apt to have even more difficulty later, when it comes to understanding the causes and corrections for your pet's problem.

When you have satisfied yourself that you have reached the "right" specialist, your chances for success are *almost* as good as they can possibly be. However, after 20 years of consultation work with dog owners, I would be failing you (and my conscience) if I didn't mention a few more precautions.

There are some impressive "silver tongues" in this field. They are exceptionally good at using the telephone interview to gain a pet owner's confidence and a preliminary meeting. To avoid getting involved in something that may not be satisfactory for you or your pet, hark back to the consultant's description of the actual programs and watch out for the following:

- *Beware of anyone who says that they can "do it for you."* Ask them to meet you at the local lake or river and see if they also walk on water. If they can, check for barely submerged rocks.
- *Watch out for anyone who says you will be meeting with their "assistant," and that they (the specialist) will supervise.*
- *Watch out for people who lead you to believe the program is going to be "easy."* Solving a pet behavior problem is rarely simple. It requires your mental effort and often some emotional adjustments on the part of all family members.
- *Watch out for someone who tries to make you feel guilty about your pet's problem.* The problem is the result of interactions between your pet and its people, plus other elements in our environment. Anything you have done that helped create the problem was done without harmful intent. No guilt feelings are warranted, only a resolve to eliminate the problem.

PART II

Correction Programs for Behavior Problems in Dogs

RMM's engaging **cartoons** are the only thing that will keep you from falling asleep in 15 minutes if you try to read this section as if it were a "book." There is a lot of repetition, because the basis for correcting so many problems involves some of the same basic procedures. However, I did not want to leave out any of the elements, because you will be referring to the *individual* program as you go through it with your pet.

Read your problem correction program as if you were going to have to take an oral examination on it. That way you will commit it to memory and put every element to work. Each correction program has been used successfully by hundreds of thousands of dog owners, who have received pamphlet versions of these programs through their veterinarians (BehavioR$_x$ Series, by William Campbell). With patience and optimism, you can have a pet that adds joy to your life.

"Poop 'n Scoop!"

Housetraining

Believe it or not, teaching a puppy or even an old dog to use a special toilet place is a lot easier than you might think—if you use this method. Why? Because my approach is natural for your dog. Thousands of dog owners have used the program successfully with me. So can you, if you will follow the dirctions strictly.

BE A TEACHER

Keep two points in mind: First, dogs are able to learn from five weeks through old age. Before they can learn, however, they have to realize that you are going to *teach* them!

Secondly, all dogs are naturally hygienic. In early life they seek a spot to eliminate that is remote from where they eat and sleep. We people are the culprits who force them to violate this hygiene. We place doors and other barriers between them and a proper toilet area.

During this program you will use two types of rewards: verbal praise and petting. Tidbits are out. We want the pet to learn for *you*, not food.

141

To make you the teacher we will use your pet's need for praise and petting, because this is natural.

How many times a day does your dog ask to be petted? I'll bet it is more often than you realize. I will also bet that you respond to its requests by petting, which is only natural. Now, however, we will use these "magic moments" to teach the dog that you are a teacher as well as a petter. Here's how.

Each time your puppy or dog asks for petting, respond by holding your hand, palm up, about a foot above its nose and saying, "Rover, sit." (Use *your* dog's name, of course.) Move your hand back over its ears as you speak. This makes the dog look up, which is the first part of sitting for our canine friends. Keep repeating "Good sit" until the dog sits. Then pet it on the throat and chest with your other hand for a few seconds as you repeat the praise.

If not achieved the first time, repeat the process until success is reached. When the dog sits for about five to ten seconds, release it from the command by saying "OK," then pet and praise again. Gradually increase the time during the Sit until you have reached one or two minutes before you say "OK." Be sure everyone who lives with the pet follows this procedure during and even after your program. Consistent treatment from the whole family makes a better adjusted, happier pet.

DIET AND FEEDING

Feed at least twice a day. All dogs do not have the same digestive rates. You may have to feed a puppy up to five times daily to avoid overloading its system and causing loose, uncontrollable bowel movements. When you find the right schedule the result is a dog that eats and then, within a few minutes, has a bowel movement. This works out perfectly because someone must be there to feed the dog anyway, so supervision to its toilet spot is not inconvenient.

How much should you feed? Only enough to produce a formed, firm stool that you can pick up with tissue without leaving any residue. If the stool is too loose, cut down by 10% steps until a firm stool is achieved. If too dry, increase by 10% steps until the proper stool is obtained.

If you see mucus or blood, or if the stools do not firm up, consult your veterinarian at once.

Do not switch diets without the veterinarian's advice. Extensive testing has proved that dogs fed varying diets are more nervous, suffer more illness and die younger. Do not short-change your pet's opportunity for a full life.

Feed inside the house. Remember, dogs are loathe to eliminate where they eat. If your dog is urinating or defecating in a certain indoor area, try feeding it right at that spot (after cleaning it up, of course). Leave the food dish at the spot between meals for a few days as a reminder against soiling that area again. Some older dogs that urinate in the house may require this food-dish treatment for up to six weeks to break the habit, but it works wonders when applied with the entire program.

WHERE TO GO

Immediately after your dog finishes its meal, "scat" it out good naturedly to its toilet area, ahead of you if possible. Then stand still and let it sniff around for its preferred spot. The act of sniffing seems vital as a warm-up to elimination. Do not interfere by urging your pet to perform.

When the duty is performed, crouch down and point at the urine or fecal matter and say, "Good dog." Look right at the stuff, not at the dog. If the dog sniffs it, praise and pet enthusiastically before going back inside with your dog.

The foregoing routine should be followed after each meal for adult dogs, on the following occasions for puppies:

- After waking up, even from a nap
- After extreme excitement
- After drinking water
- After prolonged chewing on a toy, etc.
- If it starts to sniff as if looking for a spot to eliminate.

In about four days the pup or dog should automatically head for its proper place after meals or whenever the urge strikes. If it takes longer, be patient. When this becomes routine, Phase I of the program is accomplished: the pet knows *where* to go.

When and Where Not to Go

During Phase II of the program it is vital to keep feeding times as constant as possible. Do not feed at 7:30 AM weekdays and then delay it on weekends for the sake of extra sleep. You will ruin the biorhythm of the program; your pet will become anxious and break its routine.

Dogs can control their urinations up to 13 hours, depending on activity, temperature and other factors. For housetraining, just as with children, they must learn to "clamp down" to control their eliminations. Once learned, self-control is automatic. To help them, Phase II requires that you do *not* let them out to the toilet area at times when you are not normally home to do so. Little can be accomplished teaching your pet to control itself Monday to Friday if you let it out constantly Saturday and Sunday!

Whenever you see that the pet wants to "go" during the taboo hours, distract it by tossing a ball, playing with a toy, or any activity that will take its mind off the urge. This technique can succeed in three or four days with puppies. An older dog may take a bit longer. Apply the program consistently and you will win. Clients with dogs over ten years old have succeeded. So can you.

Night Supervision

If it is possible, have your pet sleep in a room with people. This promotes fewer night accidents. Dogs are inclined to become attuned to the sleeping times of their people. Given a little blanket as a bed, most dogs sleep the entire night through.

The dog's second best friend is a doggy-door. If it is practical in your situation, get one. It can speed up the program significantly.

Secret Clean-up

Old-fashioned housetraining methods tell us to grab a pup or dog, stick its nose in or near a mess and scold or punish it physically. This kind of treatment is not necessary and may even slow down your program.

Instead, if an accident is discovered, just say "Ugh" disgustedly and whisk your pet out to its proper toilet area. Leave it there while you clean up the mess. Make sure the dog cannot see you cleaning up the urine or fecal matter. Strangely, many animals find it rewarding to witness their people picking up their stools or urine. They often leave another "present" at the next opportunity. I call this little game "poop 'n scoop." They poop and their people scoop. Let the pet watch you clean up its own, *proper* toilet area for this reason.

Indoor accidents can be cleaned effectively with a 50/50 solution of tepid water and white vinegar. This neutralizes the residual odor. On carpets, sponge out the area by stomping paper towels underfoot until dry.

Special Steps

If your dog is sneaky about urinating in the house, it may be advisable to take up its water between meals and at night. However, consult with your veterinarian.

If accidents occur only at night, try hanging a small bell on the pet's collar. This will wake you in the night. Then send the dog back to bed.

* * *

Now that you have read this program once, read it again. Keep it handy for reference. Make sure all those living with the pet follow the program closely. If the steps are taken properly, you should expect a fastidious puppy or adult dog in four days to six weeks, depending on your situation.

Remain optimistic and good-natured throughout your program, and you will be the ideal teacher during your lives together.

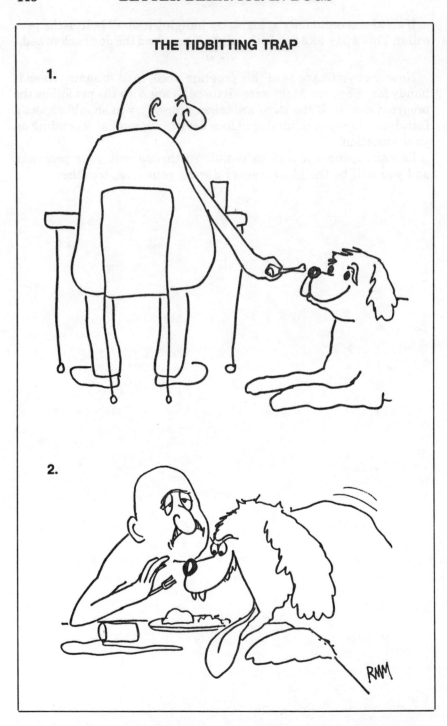

THE TIDBITTING TRAP

1.

2.

Feeding

NUTRIENT REQUIREMENTS

The dietary needs of a dog are the most misunderstood aspect of pet ownership, bar none. And no wonder. A few generations ago, dogs were fed leftovers from the family table and seemed to thrive. These usually included a little meat, some potatoes, greens, even bits of fresh salad—all the protein, carbohydrate, fat, fiber, minerals and trace elements a dog needed to remain strong and healthy.

Then came modern food processing and the introduction of canned or otherwise preserved dog and cat foods. Some companies told us our dogs needed meat, while others claimed a balanced supply of protein, carbohydrate, fat and other nutrients from vegetable sources would keep Fido in fine fettle.

The power of advertising has convinced the vast majority of dog owners that commercial pet foods are more convenient, more appealing and more satisfying than table scraps, which is probably true. However, certain problems emerge from the conflict between a dog owner's desire to provide a stable, nutritious diet and the feeling that dogs also need variety to be happy.

This feeling about variety in taste-appeal, color and texture is strictly a projection of human eating habits. The fact of the matter is that dogs thrive on monotony in their diets. They retain better health, live longer and are emotionally more stable eating the same complete, balanced commercial dog food every day of their lives.

On the other hand, if we occasionally make available some table tidbits, our pets can learn to love variety, too. This is where behavior problems can erupt; the dog may turn up its nose at commercial food or start to beg for people-food, much to the dismay of the family at the dinner table, especially when there are guests.

Begging and Finickiness

If you are plagued by a finicky eater or a begging dog, follow this program and you should clear up the problem within about two weeks:

• Feed your dog's regular diet twice daily.

• If you do feed leftovers, place them in the dog's regular food dish at its regular feeding time and delete the amount of normal food equal to the amount of leftovers. If you can, stop feeding leftovers altogether. The dog will be better off for it.

• Before you sit down to eat, walk to a spot away from the table, but where the dog can see the table, and call the dog. When it arrives there, pet and praise it and tell it to Stay. Even if you have to repeat this process many times during the meal, do it until your pet stays at that spot for the entire meal.

• When you have finished your meal, go over and praise the dog again away from the table. This will establish a happy ending for its self-control.

Follow this program until your dog simply goes naturally to its spot and remains there for the entire meal. Before two weeks have passed, even in the most stubborn cases, success should be achieved with this program.

OBESITY

Obesity in dogs can be attributed to one major cause: The pet is receiving too much of the wrong kind of food for its metabolic type and activity level. I have seen littermates proceed through life, one of them eating less than 60% of the same type of food as its brother, yet maintaining the same body weight. Each dog's system is unique. A little bit of starch may put weight on one animal, while another may burn rather than store the same starch.

If your pet is fat, consult with your veterinarian on a diet that will suit its individual metabolism, then stick to the diet for at least six weeks before you expect to see any dramatic changes in weight. Even if your dog seems wildly hungry, hold steady to the new diet. If it has been overfed in the past, several weeks must pass before its stomach shrinks to normal size. In the meantime it is normal for the dog to seem hungry all the time, since its stomach is still feeling unfilled, even though all the required nutrients are going into its system.

Keep in mind that fat dogs are the victims of our mismanagement of their diets. We hold their health and longevity in our hands. This means that any tidbitting must be stopped, in fairness to the pet. A dog of normal weight may outlive an obese pet by as much as 40%. A little human self-control can lead to many more years of delightful companionship with a healthy dog.

STEALING FOOD

Stealing food is as natural to dogs as any of their other more primitive behaviors. Historically, dogs are scavengers. Wild dogs specialize in teaming up to steal carcasses from other predators. I have seen domestic pets eat hideously rotten garbage as if it were the most delicious meal they ever had! On the other hand, I have seen dogs who did not appear tempted by a plateful of T-bone steaks, even though people were not around to control them.

If you are unfortunate enough to have a food-stealer, resign yourself to the fact that you will have to take careful precautions to control the problem. You have probably tried most of the traditional punishment and scolding routines, so it is best not to continue with these unsuccessful approaches.

There is one procedure that has worked well in many cases. It avoids physical punishment, but takes advantage of events that dogs may find unpleasant.

Follow the first two steps regarding feeding and diet mentioned earlier.

This system depends on your ability to discover your dog's "pet hate." Once discovered, this is used in association with food placed in spots where your dog may try to steal it. An example best illustrates the system.

Pet Hates

A Norwegian Elkhound had the upsetting habit of raiding the hors d'oeuvre tray when the family had guests, the only occasions when food was on the coffee table. This dog's pet hate was getting its nails clipped. The owners were advised to keep the clippers handy. Each time the dog so much as looked toward the tray, they called it to them, near the tray, and pleasantly clipped a toenail. Before they had finished a pawful of nails, the dog actually went to a corner and remained there as if riveted whenever the lazy susan was produced!

Another case involved a giant German Shepherd that hated to be bathed. The same routine was followed, except each time food was left around, the bath water was turned on and the dog was called toward the food and then toward the bathroom. One week later, after five such sessions, the owners had the sweetest smelling, cleanest non-food-stealing pet in the neighborhood.

Some other "treatments" have used ear and/or eye cleaning, putting on or taking off a collar, even going out on a cold night.

Whatever your dog abhors, barring physical punishment, apply it to this system for at least two weeks for results that will be permanent. But remember, you still have to be careful about leaving morsels around when you are not there to oversee the situation.

One treatment I *never* advise is putting the dog out of the area, in isolation. This risks establishing an association between guests and being cut off from the family. Jealousy of guests, rather than avoidance of food, can result.

During any of the procedures involving food, remain good-natured, optimistic and be patient with your dog. Behavior changes associated with food are the most difficult to achieve but are well worth the time and effort invested.

"He's begging! He's disciplined *never* to touch anything on the table!"

Puppy Training

Although our title is "Puppy Training," we will also concentrate on puppy *learning*. Training involves our conscious efforts toward formal teaching. However, your puppy will learn its most important behavior when you are not deliberately teaching it. These lessons revolve around the pup's emotional reactions to life's new experiences.

EMOTIONAL DEVELOPMENT

The first visit to your veterinarian helps shape lifelong responses to treatment. If it whimpers or cries when receiving a shot and you act upset or overly sympathetic, the puppy will get the emotional message that there really *is* something to be upset about. On the other hand, if you act happy, as if there is nothing to be worried about, the pup will minimize its own concern and follow your emotional example. This tendency holds true especially during the ages from about five to 13 weeks. It is vital in developing a healthy personality to expose your puppy to all sorts of people, babies, and other animals during this period. If you act as its emotional guide, you will help form a well-balanced pet in later life.

For instance, when you have to leave your puppy alone and you express concern while leaving, the pup will feel upset because you are. Then when it is alone, emotional tension builds up, and yelping, chewing, housesoiling or other problems can occur.

Leader vs. Follower

As important as emotional development is, a pup also needs to learn simple commands like Come, Sit and Stay, if only for its own safety. All dogs are capable of being leader or follower. Leader-pups become extremely frustrated because they cannot open doors, get their own food, etc. A happier pup is the one that accepts its people's direction—a follower.

Test your puppy to see whether it is a leader or follower type. Take it out to an open area and walk away from it. Chances are it will follow you. If it does, say "Good Dog" and crouch down to attract it to you.

If it does not follow, try running away from it and crouch to praise if it starts toward you. Try to perform this exercise daily for about two weeks in all sorts of situations.

If the puppy does not follow and actually resists any display of following, this little ritual can help achieve a better follower. Gently roll the pup on its back, holding it in that position with one hand on its chest. The puppy may struggle, yelp and otherwise resist the restraint. However, calmly persist until your pup quiets down and remains still for a moment. When this happens, release it and give it lots of praise and petting. By doing this daily you will find the puppy accepting and even enjoying its submissive position a little. Also you should notice that it will start following you when you take it out for its open-area exercises.

What's in a Name

Out of all the words your dog hears you utter daily, how is it to learn that any particular word is meant for it? The answer is simple: Just say the pet's name before any command word! For this example, let us name our puppy Skip. What should "Skip" mean to him? It should mean, "Pay attention to me because I am about to say something important to you."

But if we chat with each other, saying, "Skip did this or that today," the pup soon requires that we change our tone or volume to gain his attention. Here is a tip that can guarantee lifelong instant response to your dog's name: Use a nickname when you are talking *about* your puppy, and use the real name when talking *to* it.

TEACHING COME

Now let us teach Come. Take your pup to an area that is fairly open, but free of strong distractions. Go to the center of the area and watch the puppy closely. The instant he takes his eyes off you, call, "Skip, COME!" Immediately crouch down, turn sideways to the puppy, clap your hands and gleefully praise, "Good dog, Good dog, Good dog." Keep up the praise and clapping until Skip comes all the way to you. Pet sincerely but briefly, then stand up and step away *behind* the puppy.

If his attention does not stay on you, instantly call, "Skip, COME," again and repeat the entire procedure. If Skip gets distracted, repeat the call and the praising-crouching procedure.

Continue until Skip will not leave you no matter where you walk. Then stop that teaching session. Do not hold another for at least two-and-one-half hours, otherwise you will be overdoing it.

For the second and following sessions, either create more distractions in the first area or go to a new area.

Hold three daily sessions at the most for six weeks. In between do not use "Skip, COME!" unless a panic situation arises wherein life, limb or property may be in danger. In less serious instances when you need Skip to come to you, merely say "Skip" and then crouch, clap and praise. These nonemergency times do not require the full "panic" command, and to use it then might wear out the effectiveness of the full command.

Teaching "Come"

TEACHING SIT

Sit is the simplest thing to teach a pup. The difficult idea to get across is when to quit sitting! In other words, now that Skip is sitting, how long should he remain so? To communicate the total idea that Sit means to sit until I give you permission to get up, proceed by gradually lengthening the duration of the sit.

To achieve the sit portion of the command, first call, "Skip, Come!" using the full panic command in an undistracting area. When Skip arrives, pet and praise, keeping your left side toward the pup. Then, as you rise to stand, take your left or right hand and stroke under his chin upward to a spot over his head, so Skip must look up and a bit back to keep watching that hand. As you do this, say "Skip, Sit."

Praise instantly if Skip keeps looking up at your hand. Lean a bit backward yourself, but do not loom over the dog. If Skip does not sit down, merely repeat the "Skip, Sit" and again make the over-the-head movement with your hand. The instant he sits, lean down and pet on the chest and throat, praising verbally as you do.

After about five seconds of sit, say "OK" and step away from Skip to communicate that he can now move out of the sitting position. Crouch down and praise and then keep repeating the entire procedure until Sit is achieved on the first command. In this first session ask only for five seconds in the sit. In the next, try for ten seconds and keep doubling it until you have reached about five minutes.

If the puppy starts to lie down by your side after longer times have been achieved, do not correct or reprimand at this stage in the process. Remember, first it is learning to sit and remain in that place for some time.

Once sitting for five minutes has been achieved, you may then correct the lying-down behavior by using your hand movement to counter it the instant Skip shows a sign of beginning to lie down. Verbally praise the puppy when he corrects himself, which will be very quickly if you use this method.

TEACHING STAY

Once again using movement as the communicator, start in nondistracting surroundings with Skip, Come, Skip, Sit, and then say "Stay" as you abruptly bring your left palm from a position about a

foot in front of the pup's nose to a spot about one inch from his nose. Stop your hand abruptly. As it stops, step forward with your right foot (with the pup at your left side, the right foot is less apt to draw Skip forward) and face the puppy. Now you are confronting each other. This tends to keep Skip frozen in this Sit-Stay. Remain out front for only five seconds and then pivot back to Skip's side. Then, step forward with your left foot and say "OK" and release. Just as with Come and Sit, proceed to teach in easy steps, with minimum distractions at first, then to different areas and greater distractions over a period of six weeks.

If Skip starts to break the Sit-Stay, avoid harsh corrections or manhandling. Just rush back to the exact spot Skip started the Sit-Stay, call him back and start over. Avoid punishment and negatives to retain your position of positive leadership.

Health and Behavior

Regular veterinary checkups and routine inoculations may seem to have nothing to do with the behavior of your pet. However, dogs, cats and other pets are more likely to develop behavior problems when they have a physical problem. When you or I feel a nagging pain, whether in a tooth, an ear or our stomachs, we have the freedom to visit our dentist, otologist or general physician. Not so with our pets. Unless that nagging pain is accompanied by a swelling or eruption, or hurts so much that the animal cries out, it is doomed to suffer in silence.

REGULAR EXAMINATIONS

Our animals can react to physical problems very much like people. They can get irritable, become withdrawn or easily excitable, but they also may start to urinate too much, over- or undereat, chew themselves or other things, bark excessively, or exhibit other unusual behavior. The only defenses against the behavioral side effects of less-than-good health are regular examinations by the one individual with the qualifications to declare an animal fit—your veterinarian.

During the years I operated a full-time behavioral consulting service for pet owners, it was a policy that clients have their pets examined before starting any course of correction for a problem. This policy sprang from hard experience, not accident. A case illustrates the point.

Many clients brought dogs to me that did not appear able to settle down, along with other complaints ranging from biting to housetraining problems. Dealing with the main complaint was hopeless. The dogs, for the most part, were absolutely uncontrollable. Not only were I and the clients unable to control them; the dogs themselves seemed incapable of any self-control. Their every waking hour was spent in activity.

During this time some extremely important work was being done at The Ohio State University's department of biopsychiatry by Professor Samuel Corson, who was working with dogs showing the same hyperactivity as were some of my clients' dogs. Through proper veterinary examination, more than 3% of my clients' pets were discovered to be hyperkinetic, similar to the hyperactivity being diagnosed in children. After proper medication, the behavior of such dogs changed dramatically, making them easy to handle and a pleasure to live with. Where many clients had considered euthanasia, even if privately and with remorse, they instead gained what they called literally "new dogs."

NUTRITION AND BEHAVIOR

The saying "He went bananas!" to describe someone acting nutty, didn't get invented by a joke writer. Certain people do become "hyper" and even act mentally deranged after eating a banana. This is because of a sensitivity some people have to a certain chemical in bananas. I've never seen a dog eat a banana, but I have seen many who were called hyperactive. Also, after consulting with their veterinarians about changing their diets, I have seen many of these wild-eyed, overexcitable animals become calm, sweet, normal pets.

Like people, dogs can have all sorts of food allergies, and these can affect more than skin and coat condition. So, if your dog is "high strung," ask the doctor about trying a nutritional approach to the problem. There are now several hypoallergenic diets on the market. Also, diets higher in protein than popular commercial brands can be obtained or easily concocted in the event your dog is carbohydrate-sensitive, as are many people.

Once you and the veterinarian discover what element is triggering the overactivity in your dog, you'll be astounded by the change you will witness!

PHYSICAL AILMENTS AND BEHAVIOR

The results of proper diagnosis and treatment of a hyperactive animal are dramatic, but no more vital than diagnosis and treatment of some very common health problems. The following table lists some common physical ailments and related problem behaviors.

PHYSICAL PROBLEM	ASSOCIATED BEHAVIOR PROBLEMS
Urinary tract infection/inflammation Vaginal infection/inflammation	In-house urination; sexual mounting; self-mutilation; biting; chewing; false pregnancy; digging; barking; masturbation
Anal sac impaction—mild	House-soiling; aggressiveness; self-mutilation; overexcitability; barking; escaping; biting
Pancreatitis	Eating stools; poor learning; self-multilation; chewing; overeating; house-soiling
Visual problems: cataracts, optic nerve inflammation, brain-related causes and visual/motor complications.	Biting; fighting other dogs; aggressiveness; shyness; fear of objects, people, sounds; escaping; running away; chewing; poor learning leading to housetraining problems; self-mutilation
Hip dysplasia	Biting; shyness; self-mutilation; chewing; aggressiveness
Dental problems	Chewing; barking; biting; self-mutilation; digging; poor eating
Ear infections/deafness	Barking; biting; moodiness; chewing; lack of obedience; housetraining problems

There are many other health problems that affect behavior, but these listed usually go undetected by owners, especially in milder forms.

Nutrition affects behavior.

The Key—Your Pet's Doctor

It requires years of experience based on proper veterinary education to detect, then treat these and the more common pet ailments that can affect animal behavior. Seemingly simple problems such as intestinal worms, a condition tolerated all too often by pet owners, can affect the tissues and functions of the nervous system. The microscopic larvae of certain kinds of these pervasive parasites can and do penetrate the brains of dogs and cats. Often there are behavioral changes before we even notice the physical effects of such illnesses. A simple stool sample and regular examination are our pets' only protection against such ravages. However, the dog or cat cannot order it done; it is up to you and me.

Leash-Straining

If your dog acts as though a leash is a challenge to its freedom or a signal that the daily sled-pulling session is underway, there are some principles of body language that can correct the problem. The same holds true for balky dogs or puppies who resist moving at all.

CAUSE AND EFFECT

Most leash-strainers are pulling on a taut leash in *response* to the leash's getting taut. It follows that if you never let the leash pull on the dog, it can't pull back. This is easier said than done, unless you can run faster than your dog. So start this correction routine in a confined area such as the backyard, then graduate to more open areas when you have things under control.

Learn to Jerk

Take your six-foot leather leash and tie it securely to something solid at a spot about the same distance from the ground as your dog's collar would be. Then, holding the leash in your left hand at about the four-foot length so it hangs slightly loose, practice quickly jerking and instantly releasing the tension. Repeat this until you do not feel any tug, but only an instant's tension. Spend at least five minutes getting this down, because if you tug or pull on the dog, the problem can get worse.

Now, hook up the dog, keeping two feet of the leash in reserve for slippage. Hold the leash in your left hand, and with your left side toward the dog, start walking in a straight line forward. If your pet starts to go ahead of you, immediately do a left U-turn, cutting it off, and head the other direction. Let the leash stay loose and slip through your grasp if it starts to get tight. Praise the dog and pat your left thigh to give it a target and to hold its attention, but keep walking. Remember, you are leading.

If the dog gets so far ahead that a left turn is impossible, take a right turn (not a U-turn) as you quickly *jerk* the leash, praise, pat your thigh and keep moving until the next correction is required. The right turns can be U-turns as soon as your dog keeps up with you more readily. Remember to let the leash slip through your hand if it starts to get tight.

Make the session brief—no more than ten minutes—even if 100% success is not achieved. End it on a correct response and praise your dog profusely.

BALKY DOGS OR PUPPIES

Most balky dogs are either young or have had some bad experiences with leashes. However, the method for building their confidence is the same. It may test your patience, but the results are worth it.

From a position with the dog on your left side, with both of you facing the same direction, sudenly step forward about four paces. Do not hold the leash, but just let the dog drag it. If the dog starts to move with you, praise it, pat your left thigh and keep moving, taking shorter, quicker steps, which will help hurry the dog. If the dog catches up, stop, crouch with your left side toward it, and praise and pet lavishly.

Getting It Moving

If the dog balks totally, simply crouch, clap and praise happily. This should bring it to your side for more praise and another try at starting out. Keep repeating this for three successful approaches, then take the leash at full length and do it again. Don't let the leash pull. After a few successes, the dog should start moving with you, and you are on your way for longer walks. In the early stages of this routine, some balky dogs require that you actually *run* away from them to get them moving.

If your dog starts to grow roots and doesn't move for any of these inducements, try the run-away, crouch and clap routine. Then stand up and run a half-circle with your left side toward it and crouch, clap and praise from a position directly *behind* the dog. If the dog starts to turn with you while you're running the half-circle, praise it and pat your left thigh. Be sure that during your circling you do not approach the dog or you'll be communicating the wrong idea. If anything, gradually work *away* from it.

Puppies seem to have a critical field of vision in this balky dog problem. Unless you get far enough away, where they cannot see you

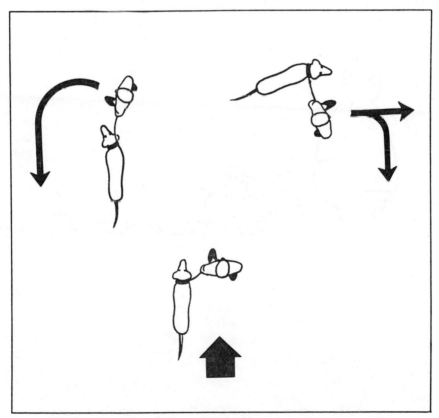

A 180-degree left turn—in front of the dog—should be made when the dog begins to move ahead. If the dog is already ahead of the trainer, a 90- or 180-degree right turn accompanied by a jerk on the leash is necessary.

clearly, they seem content to sit there. The critical distance can be up to 30 feet with pups less than three months old, and farther in some cases.

Professional Help

If your dog is such a problem that none of this works, it is best to get professional help from someone who believes in nonyanking methods of leash-training, before tackling the problem in a class situation, where distractions can overwhelm the pet. Be sure to secure the services of someone who will teach *you* to solve the problem, rather than do it for you.

Whining

The piercing whine of a puppy or an adult dog signals some kind of discomfort, either physical or emotional. Whichever it may be, the sound is extremely grating on human ears. The cause may be loneliness, hunger, cold, or frustration, as in the case of a dog that does not get its own way.

NORMAL WHINING

The puppy that whines when left alone is behaving normally during this first experience. If the whining brings about the appearance of people, even if they punish, the odds are strong that the whining will be repeated. After all, puppies are social creatures, raised within litters, so even if a bit unpleasant, having company is often better than feeling totally marooned.

If you must isolate your pet, do not make the error of "rescuing" it by punishment, or you risk reinforcing the whining behavior.

Emotion is the most important element in the relationship between people and dogs. Therefore, if you satisfy the social (emotional) needs of your pet, the chances are good that the frustrations which formerly drove it to misbehavior will be relieved, and better behavior will result.

LEADERSHIP ROLE

The pet dog that does *not* feel the need to get its own way is a happier, better adjusted dog than one who thinks it should be the leader over its people. To fill the role of leader, every dog owner needs to exercise the needed principles daily, from moment to moment. It is a mistake to think that several minutes of training per day fulfill this need. It helps, but unless the training dovetails with a total environmental leadership role played by the dog's owners, more harm than good may actually occur. This is due to the dog's extreme sensitivity to inconsistent treatment.

If the owners spoil the dog as a matter of daily practice, but demand obedience in a 15- to 45-minute training session, it is no wonder the animals balks, is even resentful, when faced with such "Jekyll and Hyde" personalities. Therefore, the best principle is consistency.

Is your dog an isolation whiner? Or does it start its vocal calisthenics when it does not get its way? Either way, the treatment that succeeds requires the pet to learn-to-earn its praise and petting, from all those living with it. It is useless for one family member to assume the "heavy" role, practicing leadership principles, while everyone else spoils the animal. More confusion results, once again due to inconsistency.

Teach to Earn Attention

The principle is easy to recite, but requires extreme self-control to practice. Each time the dog asks for attention, or anyone feels like petting it, some function must be performed by the dog. For instance, if the dog approaches and nudges a hand for some petting, the person must, very pleasantly, ask the pet to Sit, and then praise and pet it, but only for three to five seconds. All prolonged petting (fondling) must be stopped for your program to succeed.

This practice must be adopted by everyone. Within one to four days you should witness a pet that is more relaxed, actually anxious to please and less likely to get upset when denied something it wants.

Some ultraspoiled dogs withdraw from social contact when the full impact of this program is first appreciated. They actually pout. If this occurs, just let it happen. Do not press your desires or attentions on the pet. Pouting is great self-therapy. In a couple of days the dog will be back, asking for its rewards of praise and petting. Then the program may be launched fully.

Earn-your-praise-and-petting should be practiced at least six weeks and preferably for the life of your dog.

Defuse Emotion

If whining occurs only when the pup or dog is isolated, avoid such isolation if possible. If you cannot avoid it, then be sure not to make a fuss over the pet when you put it away or release it from isolation.

For instance, if the dog whines when left in the car, defuse all emotion when you get out of the car. If the dog becomes excited when you return, just ignore it. This is not simple because we all feel flattered that our pets would miss us so. Therefore, we perceive some social obligation to acknowledge the dog's uproarious greetings. Not so: Overemotionalism created the problem, so the correction requires nonemotionalism.

The same procedure should be used wherever the dog does its whining at home, inside or out. Coupled with the overall environmental program, this routine will bring success in from four days to six weeks.

Car Whiners

Some dogs whine intolerably during car rides. Once again, the leader-type animal is the basis for the problem. It cannot control the course of events (drive the car) so it builds tensions due to this frustration, then relieves (or at least tries to relieve) the tension through whining.

If you have this problem, the help offered by the general environmental learn-to-earn portion of the program should be appreciated. Nothing is more exasperating than trying to cope with a car-whiner. However, there is one aid I have found helpful—ear muffs or plugs. These allow some peace of mind for the driver and passengers and make it more bearable to ignore the whining, or to seem to ignore it.

The last thing to do with a car-whiner is to stop the vehicle. Stopping is just what the dog is ordering, next to getting out of the auto, which is its ultimate desire. So just muff-up and bear it! When used together with the general program, you should succeed in a few days to weeks.

One final word: If your dog whines only when it lies down, gets up, or otherwise moves about or even when still, consult your veterinarian before instituting any correction. If there is some genuine physical discomfort involved, such as hip dysplasia or intestinal parasites, medical attention is the first step.

During every aspect of the program, keep calm, display good-natured optimism and you will wind up with a pet that is a pleasure to be around.

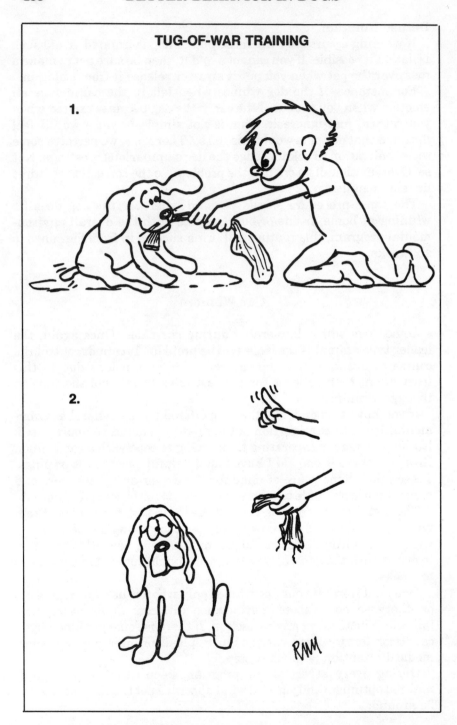

TUG-OF-WAR TRAINING

1.

2.

Chewing

If your pet is chewing up things, chances are you have already tried most of the standard remedies such as scolding, spanking and shaking the dog, but without success. One of the worst things about punishment methods is that they tend to create a breach in your relationship with your pet. The program you are about to put into action avoids all harsh physical punishment and will actually strengthen the bond between you and your puppy or older dog.

EARLY CHEWING

Puppies usually chew for the same reason human babies chew—to experience the taste and texture of the environment through the oral senses. This is normal developmental behavior for both species. The trouble is, pups have razor-sharp little teeth, which can do more damage than babies' teeth. The pup and older dog deserve the same safety precautions as the baby; put all valuable or dangerous things out of reach. Then give the pet something it will enjoy chewing. Flavored nylon bones, hard rubber balls, and safe squeaky toys are good.

Thousands of case histories have persuaded me to avoid giving things like socks to problem chewers. Dogs cannot differentiate old

169

socks from new socks, or sock materials from sofa material. Young or old, it is best not to tempt them.

To avoid making your pet mouthy, it is a good idea to treat tug-of-war like the plague! It can mouth-orient the animal, so when it misses you it will seek to chew things that remind it of you. Also, tug-of-war places your dog in fierce competition via its jaws and teeth with you, whom it is supposed to respect. I have met many badly bitten dog owners who indulged in tug-of-war. Avoid it!

CORRECTION PROGRAMS

One trouble with chewing problems is that the crime usually occurs when we are not there to correct it. Fortunately, however, it is what we do when we *are* at home with our pets that influences how they behave when we are *not* at home. Most of my clients find this hard to accept, until they follow this program and experience the joy of coming home to an unscathed household.

Calmness Pays

Before you leave your dog, do not spend the final minutes in a flurry of activity, such as putting things out of reach. Such behavior "wires" the pet for the hours it will spend alone. Instead, sit quietly in the area where you will leave it for at least three minutes, ignoring the dog. Then calmly get up and leave without so much as a word. You thereby set an example for your pet that is serene and unconcerned. If you speak and try to lighten the guilt we all feel about having to leave our dogs alone, you make the animal feel something is wrong. When this highly emotional message is conveyed, tension can start to build. Dogs are great tension-relievers; they often chew away all their tensions!

When you come home just reverse the procedure; ignore the dog for three minutes and then greet it, away from the area in which it has chewed up things in the past.

Don't Spoil

Now to the step that is probably the most difficult to practice. If you did not have a problem dog I would not recommend this. But the problem is there and until solved you *must* do this: Avoid all fondling!

This is not to say that you must not pet your dog, only that you refrain from the absent-minded stroke, stroke, stroke that all dog owners enjoy so much. The reason for this sacrifice is important to understand in chewing as well as in other problems.

If we spend a good deal of time idly petting our dogs, imagine how lonely and abandoned they must feel when we are away. The contrast between our presence and absence is too great. Tension results. And that tension will be relieved, very often, by chewing up things that either smell of, or symbolically represent us. Most of my clients say their dogs are spiteful and getting even for being left alone, when they chew. I tend, from experience, to think the dogs are missing their people and chewing to relieve tensions.

Petting Teaches

What sort of petting is permitted in the program? The best kind. The type that helps to create a better adjusted, happier, more loyal and enjoyable pet, no matter its age. When you feel like petting your dog or when it asks for petting, simply ask it to Sit, and then praise and pet it. This method gets your dog to do something to earn its pets. If you and everyone else in the household will follow this advice, all will gain a strong position of leadership with your pet. In turn, this creates a more relaxed and enjoyable dog.

Punishment is Counterproductive

At about this point many of my clients ask me, "What about letting the dog know that chewing things is bad behavior? What if I come home and find something ruined?"

Good questions, but most people who ask them have already tried to teach the idea of "chewing is wrong" by scolding, or worse, and to no avail. Also, going through all the antics and emotional upset of punishment only teaches the dog to become up-tight when homecoming time approaches. And that can lead to even more problem behavior. Besides, the object is not to teach the avoidance of already chewed-up things, but to avoid chewing intact articles.

Here is what to do when you find things in a mess at homecoming. Ignore it. That's right. Pay no attention to it in the dog's presence. Instead, in as calm a manner as you can, take your errant pet out of the area to a place where it cannot see or hear you fussing about or cleaning up the mess.

If you get emotional and handle the articles in the pet's presence, you actually might be practicing a behavior-reinforcing system called "negative reinforcement." You probably have seen some children who misbehave to gain attention, even punishment. I have seen the same thing over the years in dogs. So, as unnatural as it seems, ignore the mess and follow these instructions. Grit your teeth, and you will soon see the rewards.

Protecting Your Possessions

So far we have covered the causes for destructive chewing, how to minimize the effects and remove the causes, and how to avoid reinforcing bad behavior. Now let us consider one negative treatment that is useful only if applied along with the total program.

Remember, I said it is futile to try to teach a dog to avoid things already chewed up. However, it is helpful to teach it to avoid unchewed, intact articles. This is the only negative system I ever advise, and to be effective it must be applied as directed.

About 30 minutes before you are to leave the dog, take some Listerine mouthwash and lightly daub it on things you want your pet to avoid chewing. That's right, most dogs dislike its taste! Do not allow the dog to witness you applying the stuff. Follow this routine for four days and then stop, only repeating it if the dog backslides and chews things that have been treated.

The first day of this routine, and only on that first day, take your pet out of the treated area just before leaving it. Put some Listerine on your thumb and lightly daub it across the dog's nostrils, only on the outside surface. This usually produces the same type of distasteful expression that people show in the TV commercials. If it does happen, say "Good dog," so as to reinforce the negative reaction. If you do not get any reaction, do not worry. Just put away the bottle and leave your dog without fuss, as we detailed earlier. Repeat this in conjunction with the previous step only if backsliding occurs. Of course, if you have that rare pet that likes the taste, abandon the procedure at once!

A final comment about bones. If you want to leave a raw beef bone with your dog, ask your veterinarian about the practice and follow the advice strictly.

If you will follow this total program for six weeks you should achieve a solution to your chewing pup or older dog. Just be patient and remember that most chewing takes time to develop into a problem. Therefore, give some time for a complete correction.

"Don't worry, Doctor! His bark is worse than his bite."

Barking

If your dog is a problem barker the odds are pretty good that it either bothers you directly, or complaining neighbors bother you indirectly. If it is the neighbors, then the barking probably occurs while you are away from home.

Why should a dog bark constantly, anyway? Our experience indicates that most dogs bark either at some person, animal or object, or about some condition such as being left alone, isolated from people or other dogs.

It is normal for dogs to bark at animals and people entering the property or passing by. Some cities even define this as "reasonable" in their laws regarding nuisance barking. However, when the barking has become a problem it is necessary to understand why and how it started if we are to correct it effectively and humanely.

CORRECTING THE PROBLEM

To correct the problem, a two-fold program must be applied: the barking must be curtailed directly, and its cause must be dealt with. I have seen countless barking problems cleared up in a trice, simply by changing a yard-dog's situation. The dog was left inside the house!

173

Most people with yard-barkers say the dog is not housetrained or chews if left inside. If this is your case it would be easier to deal with housetraining or chewing than the barking problem. Also, if your outdoor dog has matured since displaying the house problem, you might try leaving it inside for short periods for a few days. Then lengthen the time over about a week. You may find the old problem has cleared up by itself through maturity, and your barking problem is corrected as well.

Excessive Barking

The cause for much excessive barking often stems from early, unconscious training by dog owners themselves. That is, when the puppy first shows signs of territorial defense the owners are delighted and may even urge the pet to carry on.

The best way to handle it when a pup first starts barking is to call it to you and then go to investigate the situation quietly. This shows the pup through your behavior how you would like it to behave. Of course, if something is really amiss, the pup will start barking again and the result is a dependable watchdog.

Unfortunately, many people bark back at their problem barkers, by shouting. Since this rarely works except when you are at home, all the dog learns is that you are boss-barker. When you are gone, the dog becomes boss and continues.

When your dog starts to bark in your presence, call it to you as quietly as the barking will allow. If the barking was about something you feel needs attention, go investigate, but do so quietly. "Shush" the dog if it starts to bark again. After this procedure, go back and settle down, calling the pet to you to keep it close by.

Be persistent with this routine for up to six weeks. Soon you will see the dog look to you after its first bark, and that is good watchdog behavior.

When You're Away

Correction of barking when you are not at home is more complicated. Territorial barking is natural to dogs, a part of their functional make-up. However, the dog that makes a full-time job of barking, even when everyday happenings take place, needs some other "function" to replace territoriality.

First it will be necessary to get the dog responding to you. The most effective device for this is your pet's need for approval. Therefore, whenever it approaches you for petting and attention you must ask it to do something, such as "sit," before petting and praising it. Everyone in the household must follow this plan. It will teach the dog that it must do something (function) to earn petting, praise and approval.

All fondling (prolonged petting) must be stopped or the program cannot succeed. It is a sacrifice, but the barking problem too often relates to a bossy, spoiled dog. And fondling spoils many dogs, especially barkers.

When you have used the sit-for-pet routine for about two days you are ready to make set-ups to correct the barking that occurs when you are not at home.

Sneak 'n Peek

A little detective work is now called for. When does your pet bark? Is it right after you leave home? If so, you will have to leave earlier than usual and apply the corrections to be detailed later.

Does the barking occur just before, or at the moment you arrive home? Then you will need to make arrangements to get home a few minutes earlier than normal for a few days. In either of the two situations you may need help from someone else if you cannot vary your schedule. Just be sure the person helping you understands the program.

I call this correction "sneak 'n peek." It is applied earlier than your usual time for leaving or arriving home and also on the days you do not work. Make all your usual arrangements for leaving and then sit down quietly for at least five minutes in the area where you leave your dog. Pay no attention to the dog. Get up and leave without a word, start the car and drive off down the street; do whatever makes the dog think you are truly gone.

Then sneak back to an area adjacent to the dog, but out of its sight and scenting ability (downwind, if outside). The instant the dog displays any sign that it may start barking, or if it does start, apply a "distraction." The distraction must be some sound other than your voice. The sound must be quick, less than a second in duration, to be successful. One rap on a window, door or fence usually succeeds in interrupting the dog's attention from the barking but avoids discovery of just where the distraction came from. If possible, make your observation point *behind* the dog when its attention is toward its usual barking target.

Be Patient

When the barking stops, do not praise the dog. Remain silent and repeat the distraction if the barking starts again or if you see or hear the dog getting ready to bark. Keep up this routine until your dog settles down.

This may take from a few minutes to an hour, but it must be done. If you have to go to work before success is achieved, do not worry. It will take a little longer but will eventually produce results.

You will know you are making headway when you notice the dog pick up a sound that used to cause barking, become alert, but settle down or merely whine or sniff in the direction of the sound.

If this entire program is applied for six weeks, you should be the owner of a dependable watchdog that does not bark at unimportant sounds and events, but will sound the alarm when something poses a genuine threat to you or your proerty. The sneak 'n peek portion of the program may require only one or two sessions to succeed, but the entire sit-for-pet routine must be adhered to for six weeks.

Be consistent and patient with your dog. The reward will outweigh the sacrifices you make in what is a vexing problem for all concerned: you, the neighbors and the dog as well.

Biting

Everyone recognizes biting as a serious problem and wants it corrected immediately. However, a totally successful program requires six weeks or more.

WHY DOGS BITE

The real solution lies first in understanding why your dog bit someone. Was it frightened? If so, what was it frightened of and for how long?

Did it feel threatened? What was being threatened: its territory, its physical well-being, its self-esteem?

When you have answered these you are starting on the road to a correction.

If your dog bites due to genuine fear of harm to itself, and if it otherwise is a happy, tail-wagging pet when you display happiness yourself, then a properly conducted program should correct the problem in about six weeks.

On the other hand, if your pet is a stoic and never wags its tail to show it is happy, then correction takes more time and care.

Correction of Biting

Correction of any type of biting entails more than merely doing things to the pet. It is also important to change things *around* the dog, perhaps even your own attitude or that of others.

First, everyone must sit down and discuss the first time the dog displayed either fearful or assertive, bossy behavior. How did you react to these early situations?

If the dog was fearful, did you try to reassure it with a sympathetic tone, even petting it? If so, your actions actually communicated to the dog that there really *was* something to be worried about. In other words, you did the wrong thing.

On the other hand, if you scolded or punished the dog, you also made a mistake. This is because the feeling of rejection from such treatment is very often associated by the dog with the people to whom it showed fear or aggression. Thereafter the dog may become fearful or even vicious when these or other people visit or approach it.

Other Causes

Another cause of dog bites is often the very people who get bitten. A question I always ask is, "How many times has the victim been bitten and by how many dogs?" A goodly number of cases indicate that some folks are just prone to getting bitten. Unwittingly they show fear or hostility, either of which upsets some dogs.

One way they do it is by standing stock still. Absolute stillness, especially on first meetings, is a prelude to attack in the canine kingdom.

Another victim "keeps an eye" on the dog. The result is another threat. Staring challenges the dog to be aggressive.

Others may approach dogs too frontally, too quickly, or even grab them by the necks or heads to get a "kiss."

Children, especially, often scream hysterically around dogs, which can trigger the dog to chase and bite.

Some victims blow in the animal's ear or otherwise tease it.

Unless teasing the victim is involved, your biting dog must be shown how to enjoy these situations, and the victims must learn new behavior around your dog.

In the case of the teasers I recommend that you explain the situation to them and, if they do not change their behavior, put away your dog at least 30 minutes before they visit your home. Better yet, don't even invite these people to visit.

Some dogs with hair that hangs over their eyes tend to become biters. If you have such a dog, do your pet a favor and tie the hair up or, better yet, cut it off. This will avoid visual surprises when people reach to pet or pick up the dog. Contrary to a popular myth, "hairy-eyed" dogs do not go blind when their eyes are exposed to sunlight.

Defense Reflexes

Before detailing your program we need to discuss different types of defense reflexes in dogs. When a dog feels a threat it reacts in one of three ways: toward it, away from it, or freezes. Fight—flight—or freeze. These behaviors occur only in the face of what the dog feels to be extreme threats.

Many dogs seem to belie their basic defensive behavior by acting otherwise at other times. For instance, I often see dogs that are quite vicious to nonfamily members, but show submissive behavior to the family, even when severely punished. I have also seen the opposite situation; the dog bites only family members and shows submissiveness to outsiders!

All this happens because of the way the dog "feels" about the situations. Feelings and emotions, not intelligence, probably dominate 99% of the interactions between us and our dogs.

Since it is emotional reactions that trigger biting, then all the "training" in the world (getting the dog to respond to some command) does not reach the heart of the problem.

Though you and all those around the dog will have to get your dog to Sit before being praised or petted, this serves only to make the dog function for its praise. In other words, it orients your dog toward your position as leader.

The Jolly Routine

The key to gaining new emotional reactions to formerly threatening circumstances lies in the Jolly Routine. It requires you to take your dog into the situations that make it feel threatened. At that instant you must introduce the device that causes happy feelings. This may be bouncing a ball, acting happy yourself, speaking a phrase, jingling car keys, or any such device, so as to switch the dog's emotional response from fear or hostility to jollity. This must be repeated until the dog shows the happy behavior without having to use the Jolly Routine.

You may find the trigger stimulus for your dog's aggression or fear is the doorbell, footsteps on the walk, or the sight of a child or adult. Whatever it is, when you gain a jolly reaction to the first trigger, you may take the dog further into the situation, by careful steps, until you achieve the "jollies" all the way from beginning to end of such situations. Then go on to different people and situations to the point where you both feel comfortable in all situations.

Warning: If you do not feel confident doing this routine with your dog off-leash, but feel comfortable with the leash, then use the leash. Do not risk communicating your tensions to the dog. It can make things worse, not better.

Body Language

When you have the ability to use the leash, make sure you are standing beside the dog's head or beside the person who is helping you. If you cannot do this, find a competent, humane trainer who will teach you to do so. Do not carry out this program until you feel competent. Did you notice I said standing *beside* the person helping? When a dog sees you beside a person it perceives you as on that individual's side, in favor of that person. Body positions speak like thunder to dogs.

When you face a person the dog sees you in a position of physical confrontation. The same body language holds true between the dog and others. Many dogs relax when a person simply turns sidewise to them. This position signals friendliness. Many a dog takes reassurance if people crouch down, especially with one side to the dog.

Program for Correction

Analyze your dog's reactions to all of these aspects, then integrate them into your program for correction. Now you have the ingredients:

- All the family members discuss the history to discover the original causes for the problem.
- Pet the dog only when it has sat for you.
- Avoid fondling. (Fondling makes biting dogs feel selfish about their relationships with people and inclined to object to others coming around and interrupting this selfish relationship.)
- Find the key to the Jolly Routine for your pet and apply it the instant the trigger stimulus occurs.
- Carefully go step-by-step through the biting situations until rehabilitation is complete.

- If your dog never wags its tail or acts happy, before starting this program you must create some key to the Jolly Routine and then start the program.
- Apply the Jolly Routine daily if you can; otherwise do it as often as possible, but success will take a little longer.

PUPPY PROBLEMS

Finally, let us talk about puppies and their tendencies to bite or be mouthy with people. First, avoid tug-of-war with such pups. Do not tease them to the point that they snarl. Such treatment only teaches the pup to use its jaw and teeth with people.

As a correction for the nippy pup, pinch one of its rear feet, when it starts to nip or mouth; this works marvelously if applied properly. Dogs have a defensive reflex basic to survival when some unexpected, possibly harmful, thing contacts their feet. The reflex is to withdraw.

On the other hand, the basic biting reflex is hooked up to the body, neck and head, particularly the snout. Therefore hitting or pinching these areas stimulates more biting!

The secret with puppies as well as older dogs is consistency. Be patient as you deal with your pet and do not expect overnight success. Biting can be solved by informed, consistent treatment.

A postscript: If you have considered that neutering your pet may help your program, discuss this with your veterinarian and follow the advice strictly.

"He did not bite you! Those are just teeth marks."

Easy In & Out

Escaping

If your dog is trying to escape from the yard, the house or even the car, the odds are strong that it has succeeded at least once in its efforts. One success usually stimulates more attempts in the future.

Two basic causes create escape-behavior problems: the animal wants to get *to* somewhere, or it may be trying to get *away* from something. It would be too simple to say that every escapist is trying to get somewhere, since I have known dogs that were escaping to avoid ultrasonic burglar alarms or just the boredom of prolonged isolation.

CASE HISTORY

One case I recall vividly involved a large German Shepherd that kept breaking out through a window, even though he had a dog-door he could have used. After several window replacements and numerous veterinary visits for stitches, I was consulted. I hid behind a fence and was amazed to see a huge tomcat jump into the yard when the owners left the house for work. He stalked toward the Shepherd's dog-door, stood poised outside for a few seconds and then plunged through with a ferocious yowl.

The next instant I heard an unmistakable canine scream of terror. The crash of plate glass announced the Shepherd, airborne and on his way to a back corner of the yard, where he huddled in some bushes.

It turned out that overfeeding was the cause of this problem. Quite by accident the tomcat learned that the Shepherd never finished its morning meal.

The cat was engrossed in finishing the feast when I entered the kitchen. I let out a war-whoop and chased the offending tom out the dog-door. At last report the cat had not been seen in the neighborhood since!

FINDING THE CAUSE

The causes for escape may be simple, goal-directed behavior aimed at freedom to roam, to get to a female dog in season or, as in our Shepherd's case, some bizarre circumstances.

To determine the cause you must be motivated to investigate all the details of your dog's escape behavior. Think back to the first time it occurred. What were the elements?

- Where did the pet go?
- How long did it stay wherever it went?
- What did you do when you got it back? (If you punished it back at the house, you did exactly the wrong thing! Even if you punished it on its way out of the area, it probably did not help and may have reinforced the escaping.)

Our program for correcting escape behavior has three phases:
1. Find the cause.
2. Remove the cause as far as is practical.
3. Reshape the environment and the dog's behavior to clear up the problem.

If the cause for escaping is some attractive goal, such as freedom to roam the neighborhood, or to visit the corner store for some treats from the children, very little can be done to remove the attractions. However, if the neighbors allow their own pets to run free in the neighborhood, or if a bitch in heat is allowed out of her house, then a direct approach to these owners is certainly justified and necessary. Escaping the yard, no matter if by digging or jumping out, is extremely difficult to clear up if irresponsible pet owners allow their animals to run free.

DIGGERS AND JUMPERS

Whether or not neighbor cooperation is received, some structural changes can be made for diggers and jumpers. For diggers, plywood or sheet metal can be driven vertically into the ground to a depth of about two feet, leaving at least four inches of the piece of material above ground. This prevents the dog's digging at it, which might result in injury.

For the jumper, a sturdy ledge can be built near the top of the fence or wall, parallel to the ground and about ten inches wide. This structure makes it impossible for the dog to gain the leverage required to boost itself over the top.

If your jumper clears the entire fence or wall in one bound, a small subfence about 18 inches high can be placed about 30 to 48 inches inside the wall. This will break the dog's stride and make jumping impossible.

One of my clients took another simple approach by digging a sunken garden around the wall's inside perimeter. His jumping Irish Setter made one gallant attempt at escaping, but was totally unnerved when his final stride dropped eight inches below the level of his approach run.

Even if these measures are taken, they do not by themselves cure escape behavior. We still must reshape the environment further and pay attention to possible causes before total rehabilitation can be achieved.

EASY IN AND OUT

Dog-doors are one of the most helpful aids in escape behavior, particularly for the dog that tries to break into or out of the house. They are also useful for a dog that digs or jumps out of the yard, especially if its goal is merely to go to the front porch and await your homecoming. The dog-door relieves tension created by the monotony of periods of isolation. The freedom to go in and out of the house at will has cleared up thousands of cases of escape behavior, with no other measures being required. Some hardcore yard escapists have become content with the freedom to go into the house and lie down in a favorite spot rather than striving for freedom outside.

If your escaping pet cannot be trusted alone in the house, ask yourself why. If it chews up furniture or other valuables, soils inside, or engages in other undesirable behavior, consult the program dealing with that indoor problem. Follow those instructions to the letter, and when combined with this program, you should expect success within one to six weeks.

Many rehabilitated escape artists I have known merely needed to be inside their owner's home, with the reassuring sights, sounds and scents, to solve the dilemma.

Getting the Dog Involved

One final step in the program addresses itself to your dog's contentment. If you do not give the dog some sort of functional activity, it will invent one, such as escaping the yard or house to patrol its property or neighborhood. Therefore, to fulfill this need you will have to ask your pet at least once a day to do something simple, like Sit and Stay for you. Do not spend more than about three minutes on this. However, this simple functional activity can do more than anything else to relax your dog. You will be demonstrating your leadership. Dogs with leaders are more relaxed and at ease mentally.

Leaders also can play with their dogs as well as demonstrate leadership through the simple Sit-Stay exercise. Get a ball, a toy bone or some article you can toss. Throw it, run with it (avoid tug-of-war if the dog has a chewing problem) to get the dog involved chasing the ball or toy. Spend no more than five to 15 minutes in play and you will be satisfying another basic canine need—the need for exercise and the feeling of joyful abandon that comes only through play. This releases tensions in the animal and increases its contentment as discussed earlier.

Do not take the dog on walks in the neighborhood, since it will extend its sense of territoriality. The playtimes will give it all the exercise it needs, anyway.

If you follow the program faithfully you should expect success within days or by six weeks, depending on your pet's personality, your own attention to detail, and the severity of the situation. If you have difficulty, re-read the program and investigate whether you might be inadvertently missing some of the elements involved. Thousands of others have succeeded by applying the program diligently. When you have adapted it to your circumstances, you should have a reformed escape dog, and a lifelong companion that is a joy to own.

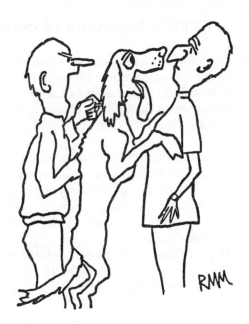

Jumping on People

The jumping dog, adult or puppy, is a social menace and a very real threat, especially to pregnant women, elderly folks and small children. If you have tried all of the generally advised corrections, such as kneeing the dog in the chest, pushing it away, scolding or maybe even stepping on its rear toes, all to no avail, this program should be welcome because it avoids physical punishment. However, to use it successfully you first have to understand why dogs jump.

FRIENDLY JUMPING

Jumping up on people or other animals takes two forms. The one we see most is what I call friendly jumping. It is usually aimed at getting up to a person's face, because this is the area that communicates verbally with the dog and also emits the essence of life itself, the breath. Dogs and many other mammals put great importance on scenting the breath of those they meet. They can identify countless different people by their breath as well as by body odor we shed into the air constantly. These airborne chemical communicators are called pheromones. People long ago lost the ability to sense them.

Other friendly jumping dogs may have had their problem unwittingly encouraged by humans. Some people love to rough and tumble with their dogs, especially puppies. But some dogs do not seem able to contain this horseplay to formalized sessions, and generalize it to jumping up on all people all the time, especially when they first meet or greet them.

The dog who cannot discriminate between when and when not to jump up needs special treatment and consideration, particularly from the people who have been playing roughly with it. The dog who does not discriminate playtime from other times can become frustrated by the seeming inconsistency of people. This frustration can be expressed by even more jumping.

The answer in this situation is self-evident: the roughhousing must be stopped. When this is done, along with the other steps I will mention later, the problem can be solved.

SERIOUS JUMPING

The second kind of jumping can be called serious jumping. In the language of the wild kingdom, dogs jump to place their forepaws on pack members to express or vie for social dominance. Our domestic pups often start this behavior with their human companions.

This type of jumping can be recognized when the dog jumps and then remains still with its forepaws on the person. The proposed underling is then supposed to remain still as well, thereby signaling submission. Since few respond this way, the dog can become upset and may jump with even more determination.

Most dogs of this type are bossy in other ways as well. To solve the problem effectively, everyone living with the dog will need to follow this program strictly. Follow these directions for sexual mounting as well.

CORRECTION

Our approach to correction is straightforward and simple. First you must spend more time with your pet, if possible. Do not throw it out of the house to avoid the jumping.

Most problem jumping takes place when a dog first meets people. To help the pet contain its enthusiasm you will have to teach it some substitute behavior that is more rewarding or less frustrating than the jumping. So, when you and others see the dog approaching, ask it to Sit as you move your hand, palm upward, over its head. This will cause it to look up, and looking up is the first part of sitting for dogs.

Tell the pet "Good Sit" when it first looks upward. Be patient and repeat this process if the sitting is not achieved immediately. When the sit does happen, crouch down and pet the dog on the throat and upper chest. Avoid petting so enthusiastically that you re-excite the dog into getting up from its sit. Your crouching gives the dog a chance to get a whiff of your breath and satisfies that urge to scent the pheromones mentioned before.

Involve Others

After a few days and experience with several people the dog will not require the crouch and will substitute the sit for jumping up.

Whenever you and others first greet the dog, avoid overexciting it. Stand with your side toward it rather than facing it. For some dogs the act of facing them stimulates jumping. One of the causes for this is people who face dogs, defensively raise their hands to their shoulders, and say "Down." Even though the voice says down, the hands are saying, "C'mon up!" Some dogs actually learn to jump up to the word Down through this unwitting training.

You cannot control all others and their movements, so you will have to teach your dog to sit when this defensive hand-raising occurs. Do this after you have achieved Sit to your spoken command. Then, ask for the sit as you raise your hands to your shoulders or chest. Expect a jump or two at first, but be consistent by countering the jump with a sidestep while you repeat the Sit command. Repeat the routine until your pet sits for the handraising without any need for a command. Then you will be ready to enlist the assistance of some sympathetic friends to follow the same procedure you have used.

After a few people have done it, you will have a pet who sits rather than jumps when it meets people. Also you will have avoided all of the bad side-effects of scolding and punishment.

Jumping on Sitters

If the dog jumps up when you or others sit down on a chair or sofa, the following technique works wonders if practiced for a few days on a regular basis. Each time you see the dog approaching with the intention of jumping up, before it is even close enough to you to jump, abruptly stand up and use the hand-over-head technique to teach Sit.

When the sit is achieved, pet the dog and then start to sit on the chair again. This is a critical moment in the plan, because your movement to sit may trigger your dog to get up. If you see this start to happen, straighten up again. The dog should settle, whereupon you must start again to sit.

This little routine can be extremely subtle. Sometimes just the act of starting to bend your knees to sit can cause the dog to start to get up or jump. So watch carefully and react instantly.

If you use body language consistently with dogs you will communicate effectively. And the better your communication, the better will be the control of your dog. Thus, from teaching your dog not to jump up, you will also gain an improved relationship with it.

Try these techniques with dogs that jump up, other than yours. As you become more expert with it you will find yourself less troubled by all jumping dogs.

Follow the program with patience and sincere dedication, and you should see success within a few days or weeks, depending on how often you put it to work. The rewards in terms of a well-mannered pet will far outweigh the effort invested.

"He chases cars, and the other day he caught a Datsun and simply ruined it!"

Chasing Cars

Most of the dogs that become bona fide vehicle chasers have extremely sensitive reflexes to chase anything that moves suddenly or quickly. If your pet has ever "caught" an auto, motorcycle or truck, you know the serious danger involved for both animal and people. The risk of injury to both parties is frightening and can be expensive. This program is designed to help you overcome the problem of chasing, as well as to advise you of the legal dangers involved.

Most communities have leash laws. Check with your authorities. Get a full explanation of the penalties and risks assumed when a dog is allowed to run freely and cause injury through chasing. The consequences have led to financial ruin for some owners. With this in mind, undertake the following program as a safeguard against a time when, through no fault of your own, your dog may get the urge to chase. It is no guarantee, but is has helped dogs control the urge, sometimes to the point of ignoring former chase-objects.

ESTABLISH LEADERSHIP

Most dogs that chase cars do so to fend off "invaders" of their territories. Others just seem to make a game of the activity. In either case, the dog needs to follow the example of a *different* behavior,

191

provided by a teacher. That leadership must come from you and others who live with the pet. The following program must be adhered to strictly if the problem is to be solved.

Your dog must learn to earn its praise and petting. To do this, you' will need to ask the dog to do something when it wants petting and when you want to pet it. For instance, if the dog approaches you happily, ask for Sit and then pet it. This little procedure will start to take effect in a few days or less. You will see the dog looking more to you for directions. When this occurs, you are ready to move to the next step in the program. If this does not occur and you do not start to feel you are in control, it may be advisable to find an obedience instructor who will teach your whole family the techniques of gaining leadership. Be sure to find one who agrees to all people living with the dog becoming involved. Having only one person in the household with the ability to teach and lead the dog will not suffice.

Remove Causes for Chasing

There are several activities that make a chaser worse than need be. These must be removed from the environment before undertaking the program.

Walks: If it has been your habit to walk the dog around the neighborhood, this must be stopped before and during the first two phases of the program.

Urination: If the dog urinates beyond its line of boundary this also must cease. Otherwise, the dog is extending its territory beyond its rightful boundaries and will continue to view cars as invaders.

Fence-worrying: If your dog has a fence along which it chases or runs, special steps must be taken to keep it out of that area.

Keep Within Boundaries

The first step to correct a chaser is to establish reasonable boundaries across which your pet should not stray. Wherever this is—the sidewalk, curb or fence—take the dog (on a leash, for safety's sake) toward that boundary, walking briskly. When within three or four feet of it, shout some word of alarm ("Watch out!") and abruptly turn around and run back toward the house or other area you want the dog to retreat to. Repeat the process until, when you approach the boundary, the dog stops and looks back, or toward you. Be sure to praise the dog each time as you carry out this procedure.

Warning: If cars, bikes or runners are involved, make sure you have the situation secure; that is, do not run the risk of having strangers at the wheels of cars or on bikes. Make all set-ups with people who are aware of the problem and will cooperate by stopping their vehicles if the dog breaks loose. Put a 20-foot extension of cord on the leash, to allow you to run back toward the safety area ahead of the dog in the initial stages. Never undertake the procedure when risk of injury might be involved.

The Final Test

When the dog no longer shows interest in chasing beyond its boundaries, the next step is to walk it deliberately beyond the boundaries in areas where chasing has occurred in the past. Make the same types of set-ups with friends as at the boundary lines, but instead of running back to the home area, simply back away with the same suddenness as before and ask your dog to Sit. Keep this up until the dog sits without your command. When this point is reached, continue the exercise about three times per week for six weeks. Do it in different areas until you are sure the dog is responding without your cues to back up and sit. When this happens, your pet has internalized the correction.

When you feel confident the dog has lost interest in chasing, you may want to resume walks in the neighborhood. This is all right, but do not allow the dog to urinate or defecate off its territory; otherwise old territorial feelings can be reestablished, and the problem may erupt again. In fairness to neighbors, joggers, drivers and bike riders, this is a small luxury for your pet to give up. The joy of a well-behaved dog that once was the terror of the street will be your reward.

CONSISTENCY IS ESSENTIAL

1.

2.

Babies, New Pets and Dogs

The introduction of a new baby or animal into the household of an established dog or cat requires some thoughtful preparation. If the established pet is normal, healthy and well-adjusted, the joy of the occasion should be reflected in its behavior—good-natured curiosity about the newcomer. There are, however, several steps that ought to be taken to ensure an emotionally upbeat tone to the proceedings.

PREPARING THE PET

Analyze the relationships between everyone in the household and the pet. Are they positive? Are the people in the family praising and petting for good behavior? What negative aspects are there in the relationships? If there is more negative than positive, then turn this around and work on the problems. An example will help explain this.

A young couple expecting a baby had a small terrier which they had allowed up on the furniture when it was a puppy, but then decided to keep off the sofa and chairs. Though they had tried all sorts of measures, including punishment, the dog would jump onto the sofa when the owners were away. This brought about a situation where the dog was scolded almost daily when the owners arrived home to

195

find it just getting off the furniture, or found telltale dog hair thereon. However, both husband and wife admitted they sometimes weakened and allowed the dog up with them, but only on special occasions in the evenings. Otherwise the relationships were excellent among them. With the coming of the new baby, though, they decided this practice should be stopped for hygienic reasons. They felt the dog might have fleas or be a carrier of some disease that could be transmitted to the child.

When the newborn baby was brought home, the terrier, quite normally, was extremely curious about it, wanting to jump up, sniff and investigate it. The parents scolded the dog and put it out of the house. The result was that the dog, a male, started urinating in the house, especially in the baby's room if the door was left open. The problem became worse as the dog was punished whenever the urine marks were found. Within a couple of weeks the usually happy dog started skulking whenever the baby was present and would not come near it. The owners became worried enough to seek professional advice.

The situation in this case appeared obvious when viewed from outside: Jealousy resulted from an association of the dog between the arrival of the baby and the disapproval, even rejection, by its cherished owners. The solution also seemed obvious, but required a change in the attitudes of the owners. The baby's pediatrician agreed that if the parents were worried about fleas and disease, the answer was to keep both dog and household flea-free. A trip to the veterinarian ensured the proper procedure was followed to get rid of any fleas and assured the parents of the animal's excellent health. This included a regular schedule of bathing for the terrier.

Besides these measures, the owners followed a program of praising the pet each time they brought the baby around or paid attention to it. They taught the dog to sit by the sofa, and held the child so the terrier could smell it—all done with happy, praising words for the situation. The result was that the pet soon wagged its tail whenever the baby got attention, since it now was a shared, totally positive attention. The urination problem disappeared overnight.

This case highlights one of the major concerns about newcomers, whether babies, animals or guests. The best procedure is to make the arrival a happy one that includes the established pet. Better yet, the arrival should mean the animal gets more, rather than less attention than before. This is where a most important step in preparing the pet is necessary.

How Much Attention

Your pet is highly sensitive to the amount and nature of attention you give it. In preparing for the newcomer, take stock of how much, and at what times you are giving attention to the established pet. For instance, if you feed it at 8:00 A.M. and 6:00 P.M. and the schedule will have to be delayed when the newcomer arrives, adjust the feeding time at least four days before that occasion. This avoids any association between the arrival and delayed feedings.

If you feel you pay constant attention to your pet, especially if it demands it, cut down on the amount of attention a couple of weeks before the new arrival. However, do not cut down on the positive quality of the attention you give the animal. If anything, intensify it; make it more happy.

If you spend a good deal of time absent-mindedly petting your dog or cat, remember that the animal will sorely miss this if it cannot continue when the newcomer appears. Jealousy could result, and problems crop up.

One of the best ways to prepare a pet that constantly demands petting is to teach it to do something for the petting, such as Sit. This is a fairly simple exercise that most dogs already know how to perform and can be used anytime. The plan is simply to ask for Sit each time the animal seeks petting. Rather than prolonged stroking, make it a brisk, upbeat, brief petting. Then, go on with some other activity. This will be especially necessary after a new baby arrives. Preparing the pet for it in this way avoids the possibility of the established animal's association between newcomer and any deprivation.

Personal Contact

How closely should a pet and new baby be allowed contact? This should be discussed with the pediatrician. The doctor knows your child, its state of health and immunization schedule. On the other hand, your veterinarian knows the state of your pet's health. A thorough examination a few days before the arrival should be scheduled. At that time any possible problems can be discussed with your pet's doctor. Thereafter, it is a matter of personal preference. Many parents are comfortable allowing their pets to enjoy extremely close contact with their babies, even sniffing and licking them. Others are more reserved. The plan that works best is one which ensures that the pet does not see the newcomer as an interloper. Rather, the interpretation should be that the newcomer means more positive attention than before the arrival. This avoids jealousy and problems.

Use Your Judgment

You are more sensitive to your pet than any outsider who offers advice. If you feel uncomfortable about introducing a new baby or another pet into the household, so will your pet. This is because your dog or cat probably has more emotional empathy (feels as you feel) with you than with any other being in its life. Therefore, if you feel that your pet is not safe around babies, do not expose the baby to situations which might be dangerous. However, avoid making your pet feel left out. For instance, if yours is an outside dog, intensify your contact with it outside. Do not let the pet feel abandoned after the newcomer arrives. Instead, make it feel it is getting more and better attention.

WHEN BABIES CRAWL AND WALK

Maturing babies not only look different when they start to move about, they also undergo changes in body chemistry and even smell different, especially to animals. The first time your baby starts crawling, the pet might be quite surprised. The animal may want to investigate the baby more closely, might show casual interest, or could even be startled and act upset about it. At this time it is up to you to show the pet how to interpret the baby's new-found mobility. Appear happy about the situation, and chances are the dog or cat will feel likewise.

When the baby starts to crawl or walk toward the pet, follow the same Jolly Routine. If your dog appears edgy about the baby's approach, good-humoredly praise the dog. Avoid scolding and grabbing the baby away. This can make the pet feel that baby needs punishing or that something is genuinely wrong with the situation.

Just as dogs like to investigate babies, there comes a time when babies want to investigate dogs. It is not wise to leave babies and dogs in an unsupervised situation where the baby might inadvertently hurt or corner the animal. Unfortunately, babies usually want to poke their fingers into the pet's ears and eyes, which is understandably upsetting to the pet.

Babies do not walk; they toddle. A dog or cat, cornered by an approaching toddler, may feel threatened and defend itself by escaping, growling or hissing (which the baby does not understand), snapping or scratching. Therefore, it is good practice to supervise the early interactions between newly mobile babies and your pets. Show your pet a happy interpretation for the baby's activities, and a better lifelong relationship will result.

Carsickness

To appreciate fully the problem of carsickness we have to project to the dog some human sensations. Dogs suffer motion sickness in the same situations as do people, and they respond to medical and behavioral therapy in much the same way. This program for carsickness has helped thousands of dog owners who have followed it. It can help you and your pet as well.

KNOW THE CAUSE

There are several causes for carsickness. One is created when a new puppy, already upset about being taken from its litter, is further upset by the car ride to its new home. If the puppy tends toward motion sickness, it will probably start salivating and then vomit. If the new owners then make too big a fuss over it, pour on too much sympathy or otherwise get upset, the puppy senses that something is genuinely wrong, and the seeds are thus sown for future carsickness.

The way puppy owners react to situations provides a model for the way the pup will react. I call this the *interpretive factor,* and it is usually more important than the fact that the puppy got sick in the first place. It is far better to ignore the carsickness than to overreact emotionally, no matter how sympathetic we may feel towards the animal.

Sensory Problems

Puppies that have been handled very little often suffer from car-sickness. In dogs and people there is an area of the brain called the vestibular center, which integrates many of the sensory impressions we receive. It is especially important in the coordination of visual, tactile (touch) and balance functions. In very young animals this brain center needs to be stimulated if proper sensory integration is to develop.

Dogs that get carsick often lack this early handling and stimulation. There has been little experience of getting picked up, turned about and cuddled upside down. Later, these dogs may tend to be carsickness victims. This is not to suggest that if you have a carsick six-month-old big dog you should start hoisting it up as part of your correction program. But if you have a pup or small breed it might be helpful if you do it gently a couple of times a day.

Visual causes are also akin to human experience. Many children who are forced to sit in the back seat get carsick. So do many dogs. However, if they sit in the front seat they are fine. It appears that when the vision to the front is restricted, as in the back seat, the objects seen whizzing by out of the side windows have the effect of causing nausea.

Bossy Dogs

The last cause to be considered also has a parallel in people. Some dogs that are bossy, leader types get upset when they cannot control many of life's situations. And the car certainly puts them out of any position to control. So, like the bossy child, they get emotionally upset and carsick.

THE CORRECTIVE PROGRAM

The first step, no matter what the cause, is to make sure the pet feels you are a competent leader. To do this, ask it to do something each time before you pet it. This can be as simple as telling the dog to sit, then petting it with lots of praise. This will transmit the message (after a few days) that you expect it to earn its praise and petting. Do not curtail your petting, but just ask for some function to be performed before you pet. It is difficult to teach your dog not to be carsick if you cannot get it to function in other ways for you.

Small Beginnings

Take the dog in the front seat of the car for an extremely short ride twice daily, just down the block and back home. While getting into the car and all during the ride you must be jolly, acting as if something good is going to happen. If your pet has a favorite ball, toy or bone, take that along and use it to sustain a happy frame of mind. Follow this routine a couple of times a day for four days in a row, if possible. Also, do it at different times of day and at night. In this way you are teaching your pet in short, happy rides that the car is not so bad at all, but a pleasant place to be.

If the dog gets sick, ignore it for the time being and do not clean up until you are back home and the dog cannot see you doing it.

When the short rides no longer produce any signs of nausea, lengthen the time and distance of the rides. Do this by five-minute segments. When you reach twenty minutes per ride you then must vary the routes you take. Try a main highway, a hilly or curved road, all the while keeping up the jollity and happy behavior.

Help from Friends

When the longer rides fail to produce nausea, have the dog ride in the back seat of the car. If your pet resists, take along another family member or friend. Warn them against coddling the dog, but have them do the Jolly Routine.

When you have reached this point the program should be carried on for six weeks with at least one car ride every other day to reach permanent success. If there is any backsliding, merely start again with the short rides and you should get things in hand within a few days.

Some dogs have special quirks relative to the direction you take them. If you find this with your dog, do not avoid going in that direction; just proceed at first for shorter distances that way. I recall a Poodle that got ill every time the car traveled in the direction of the groomer! The program of shortened rides in that direction works well in such cases.

If your dog has been on medication for carsickness, discuss with your veterinarian the method by which to wean it off the drug. Sometimes a "cold-turkey" approach works well. However, the doctor knows your dog, and the medical directions must be strictly adhered to for success.

A word about using food rewards to correct carsickness. I have found it to be disruptive. After all, it is the digestive system we need to calm down, and food only tends to excite it.

Follow this program for as long as it takes to solve the problem, which might be as long as six weeks or as short as a few days. Whatever the case, be patient and good-natured through it all, and your reward should be a pet that is a joy in the car.

"I'm the lady who called about the tranquilizers."

Fearfulness

A dog or puppy experiencing genuine fear can be pitiful or frightening to behold. Fear causes a dog to respond toward the threat, away from it, or to freeze (play possum). This program is concerned with dogs that are fearful of nonhuman factors, such as noises, sights and even certain rooms.

Through the years I have found that the things my clients felt were frightening their dogs were not always the true causes of the problem, but were signals for some other, subsequent event that the dog feared. An example may help illustrate this, and you might find it applies to your dog's problem.

CASE HISTORY

The Fourth of July holiday often brings serious problems. A typical case came to my attention some years ago involving a delightful female mixed Labrador Retriever and a family: mother, father and three teenage girls. The dog was a happy-go-lucky type and did not seem to have a care in the world. However, when at my suggestion, one of the girls, out of the dog's sight, shot off a cap gun, the dog stopped in its tracks and started to tremble violently, its eyes glazed and it began salivating streams of fluid. When this happened the family all gathered around the pet speaking sympathetically, trying to console her out of the "spell." The Labrador did not even seem to know they were there.

I then suggested we all walk around to the rear of my office building, out of the dog's sight. I asked everyone to act happy, as if we were anticipating some pleasant experience. This they did, and we had been out of sight for no more than two minutes before the dog came racing around the corner, wagging her tail as if she were expecting a most happy experience.

The Labrador had just emerged from what is often called a psychomotor seizure, one with no apparent physical cause. To help in this type of case, whether your dog shows reactions as gross as the Labrador's or simply mild fearfulness, we have to recall the first situation in which the problem was evident. In this case, the teenage girls were having a Fourth of July party when one of their guests lit a large firecracker. It exploded close to the Labrador, whereupon the dog tried frantically to get out of the area. When the girls saw this, they got hold of their pet, cuddled her and tried to calm her, but also shouted at the offending guest. While two of the girls held the dog, the third angrily pushed the boy out the door. The dog was then taken to a bedroom, the party ended, and the animal was literally cuddled in bed all night.

Never before had the Labrador been frightened of loud sounds, but from that time she appeared terrified even by car backfires.

Interpretation—Your Role

The pet reacted rather normally for her type of nervous system to the initial shock of the exploding firecracker. However, the girls provided the genuinely upsetting *interpretation* of the incident by showing the extreme reactions themselves. They literally showed their dog how to feel and react. In this case the dog responded inwardly by freezing. Other types of dogs may run in wild-eyed excitement, responding outwardly.

Step one in correcting fear behavior is to analyze your situation. Discuss the first time it occurred, how the pet reacted and, more importantly, how you and others treated the situation. When you uncover all these facts, it will become apparent that your behavior is going to be most vital in correcting your pet's problem, by providing a new interpretation for the dog.

If the dog was alone when it acquired its fearfulness you will need to be especially patient with it. This often happens when the owner works and some noise or other event upsets the dog. In this situation, it is frequently just being isolated that produces reinforcement for the fearful behavior. This applies particularly to puppies under the age of six months.

CORRECTIVE PROGRAM

Whether or not you know the details of the first fear-producing incident, the following program should be undertaken for six weeks. Do not omit any of the steps.

Every dog needs to feel it has a leader if it is to react in new ways to formerly frightening events. To achieve this, you will have to prove to your pet that you are this person. As a part of this routine ask the dog to do something whenever it seeks affection and petting. Dogs seem to cherish our approval and petting. If we ask them to do something, even as simple as Sit to achieve approval, they soon become highly responsive to our leadership.

Some dogs with hair that hangs over their eyes tend to become shy or even fearful. If you have such a dog, do your pet a favor and tie its hair up or, better yet, cut it off. Life down on the floor is tough enough without having to look at the world through a picket fence. This will avoid visual surprises when people reach to pet or pick up the dog. Contrary to a popular myth, "hairy-eyed" dogs do not go blind when their eyes are exposed to sunlight.

Avoid fondling. When you pet, make it brief and good-natured petting. Long periods of fondling can spoil the dog and ruin any correction program. On the other hand, do not command the dog as if you were a drill instructor. Speak naturally and avoid appearing threatening. In other words, do not be either a softie or a tyrant.

After two to four days of this leadership treatment you will begin to see a pet that is more eager to please, and you can then start the next step in the program.

The Jolly Routine

Make arrangements to produce the noises or situations that elicit the problem behavior from the dog. Also be prepared to produce an object or situation that makes your pet wag its tail and appear happy. Each dog has its favorite toy, or some key word, that causes it to act jolly. If yours does not have one you will need to create one. Try bouncing a ball, playing with a toy, laughing, or anything that brings forth a wagging, happy response; even the rattle of car keys often succeeds.

Now produce the situation that causes the fear behavior. But, the instant you do so, also produce the happy-type stimulus (Jolly Routine) with gusto! It is marvelously effective when carried out with conviction.

When you use it after a fear-type stimulus is produced, do not wait for the dog to get fearful. Immediately introduce the happy element. Not even one second should pass between fear and happy elements. When you apply the Jolly Routine the results should be as follows.

At first your dog may appear a little confused and even fall into its fear pattern. Even so, just keep up the Jolly Routine for a minute or two, then go on about some other business, paying no attention to the dog. After about five minutes, repeat the whole process. Do this no more than four times, twice a day if possible. Allow at least three hours between the two daily sessions. Continue the process for six weeks.

You will know you are succeeding when the dog begins to wag its tail even before the jolly business. If you see any backsliding, merely restart the program.

ISOLATION FEAR

If your dog becomes fearful when left alone, add the following element to your program. Before leaving home get all your preparations for departure completed, then sit down in the area where the fear behavior occurs. Do not pay one bit of attention to your dog. Read a paper, drink a cup of coffee or tea, but ignore the dog. After five minutes, get up and leave, still ignoring your pet, and go to work or run your errands.

When you return home you must enter without any emotional display; say "Hi" to your pet and then ignore it for at least five minutes. If there is evidence of fearful behavior, such as chewing, ignore it and clean up the mess when the dog is away from the scene and unaware of your activities. On your days off you may do this routine two or three times, but leave three hours between each set-up.

If you know that certain sounds trigger the fearfulness, produce these on your days off. However, do not produce them and then rush back into the home. Instead wait about five minutes before re-entering. By doing this you will demonstrate that there is nothing to be upset about, once again providing a leadership example.

If the dog has had tranquillizers in the past, consult with your veterinarian before starting the program. Follow instructions strictly.

Throughout the program display patience. Remember, this type of phobia in persons can take years to correct. But your dog can respond well in months, weeks, or even days.

A final caution: If your pet might do something harmful to itself or your property, take special precautions to avoid this when you plan your corrective set-ups.

Isolation Fear

"You talk about a clean dog! Victor can't stand to have his room all littered . . . so he eats his own droppings!"

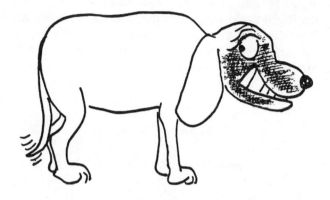

Coprophagia

Eating stools, unpleasant as it may seem, is not all that rare and not always abnormal dog behavior. The mother with new puppies eats their waste to keep the litter sanitary. I have seen famished stray dogs eating stools, probably for their slight food value.

NATURE OF THE PROBLEM

Some dogs eat their own stools because their digestive systems lack certain required elements, so they turn to their stools for the nutrients therein. This creates a vicious cycle. In these situations, carefully supervised veterinary guidance is required. The doctor's advice must be followed strictly or else the problem can persist for the pet's lifetime.

Another type of stool eating occurs with puppies. Human children often investigate their feces, and so do pups. Parents communicate their disgust of this practice through words, tone of voice and facial expressions. With puppies and even adult dogs such communication is limited. The dog can seldom be "taught" to find stools revolting. Once we recognize this, the problem can be dealt with intelligently and effectively.

Dogs who practice problem coprophagy fall into two types: those who do it at every opportunity, and those who do it only occasionally.

Dogs who eat their stools only now and then need special supervision, both in diet and toilet routine. I have seen hundreds of such cases where the stool-eating happens only after the pet is given some extra or different type of food. Their systems cannot handle the new or excess nutrient, and so pass it underdigested. Since the stool then contains nutrition, it is eaten.

Feeding Program

In all types of coprophagia, the diet must be consistent, both in quantity and content. Any changes can produce loose stools and ruin the corrective program.

The quantity of food required by dogs per pound body weight can vary so widely as to seem unbelievable. I have seen German Shepherd littermates about the same weight, one of which required one-third less of the same food than its brother per day! The clients felt that their light eater must have either physical or psychologic problems. Neither was true. In fact, the light eater outlived its littermate by fifteen months.

Watch Stools

The standard used for the amount to be fed is this: Feed just enough to produce a formed, firm stool. If the stool is loose or has a rope-like consistency, the amount fed should be reduced 10% at two-day intervals until a formed, firm consistency is achieved. Do not fear apparent underfeeding of your coprophagiac. If it begins to lose weight, consult your veterinarian. If your dog is overweight, this program may add years to its life and solve the coprophagia as well!

Feeding Frequency

Another necessity involves the frequency of feeding. You will have to feed your dog twice daily to succeed, probably for the rest of its life. Dogs hold food in their stomachs about six to nine hours after eating before it is passed into the intestines. Most of them have a natural cycle time (from eating to eliminating) of about 19 hours. Our domestic pets usually learn to control this elimination time for 24 hours, due to the human daily living schedule. This is a desirable situation, especially in cases of coprophagy. Since you have to be on hand to feed the dog, you then are also there to supervise its toilet duties as part of your program.

AVOID PUNISHMENT

If you have already tried scolding, or punishing, or rushing to pick up the stool before your dog could eat it, you may be in the predicament where the dog will no longer eliminate in your presence. If this is the case, you will have to get the dog out of its toilet area and then remain nearby as unobtrusively as possible. If the pet still will not eliminate, find some spot from which you can monitor the situation but be out of the dog's sight. Be patient until the dog does its duties.

In all coprophagia cases, after the pet finishes eliminating you must instantly introduce some highly distracting, enjoyable type of activity to take its mind off the stool. This might be bouncing a ball, tossing a favorite toy, offering a car ride, a walk, even just running happily about the area.

Whichever it may be for your pet, use it with enthusiasm. Then leave the area with your dog, praising it all the way so as to reinforce its forgetfulness regarding its stool. After a few such successful distractions, your dog will leave the stool upon finishing its elimination, with no need for your intervention. When this happens be sure to praise it happily as you both depart from the area.

Secret Clean-up

During the program and afterward, do not clean up the toilet area when the dog might watch you doing so. Dogs are clever at imitating our actions. I have seen cases of coprophagia wherein this element actually caused the problem; the dog was merely getting rid of the stool, but using a most undesirable method! It is necessary to keep the toilet area cleaned up between uses in this program, but do not let the dog see you.

I am often asked about what type of food to feed the dog that practices coprophagy. The best answer is to feed what the dog thrives on, but make sure the veterinarian agrees with the selection. The doctor knows your pet's metabolic type. Some dogs thrive on relatively high-fat diets, others cannot metabolize them. If the doctor prescribes diet supplements, follow the dose requirements exactly, otherwise the program may fail.

Stay with this program for six weeks, and you should experience the pleasure of a dependable pet that will be a delightful member of the family.

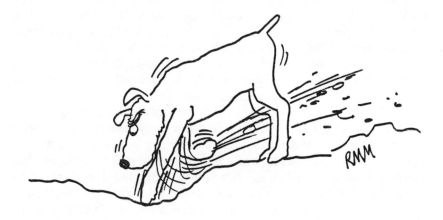

Digging

An excellent approach to the problem of the digging dog is the same that a reporter takes when gathering facts for a story. The *What, Who, Where, When* have to be documented as a first step. Then the *Why* becomes apparent.

What, is simple . . . the dog is digging. That also seems to solve the *Who.* But I often find that not only is the dog involved, but other animals and even people are part of the problem.

WHY DOGS DIG

If your dog is digging to escape from the yard to chase after or socialize with other animals or people, and if you have tried to secure the yard, you will have to consider ways to change your pet's environment to solve the problem. Ask yourself these questions:

- When does it dig?
- Is it only when left alone out there?
- If so, why do you leave it outside?
- Is it to avoid some other misbehavior inside the house?

Perhaps it would be simpler to get a dog-door or to deal with the inside problem. These alternatives deserve consideration, along with the following program.

Our pet dogs were born and raised in the intensely social environment of their litters. They are "groupies." This early life is the basis for the enjoyment we gain from our pets, as well as the problems. Some dogs cope with social isolation quite well; to others it appears to be unbearable. Those that cannot bear it often literally dig for freedom and social contacts. When these dogs are left outdoors where they can see, hear or smell people and other animals, it is no wonder that they try to get out to meet them. In many of these cases a dog-door or simply leaving the dog indoors solves the digging nicely.

Another element can be the owner who enjoys gardening. The dog is a great imitator. If it watches people digging in the garden it often takes up the practice. This can be stopped when people are home, but not when the pet is left alone. Therefore, a digging dog must not be allowed to witness gardening as a part of its correction program.

A further element is an owner who spoils the pet. Doting on some dogs when home creates a dog that may overmiss people when left alone. Therefore, isolation will cause tension. Dogs are great tension-relievers. They act out their frustrations, sometimes digging furiously. They rarely suffer psychosomatic diseases as do people. If your pet is in the spoiled category, some steps to unspoil it will be necessary. This is probably the most difficult portion of the program to put into effect.

Who's Boss?

Ask yourself what your dog does for you. Will it come when called, sit, stay, etc? Make a mental list. Then make a list of the things you do for your dog. Do you get its food, water, provide its shelter, open and close doors, groom it? When it wants to be petted do you comply?

If you find yourself at the beck and call of your dog in everyday life, is it any wonder the dog may perceive you as its servant and itself as master of the relationship? Then, when you ask it to accept being isolated from you or other living things, the "master" will find it difficult or impossible to *not* get extremely upset and try to do something about it. The picture had best be changed for the good of dog and owner.

Because our dogs are domesticated they never get the opportunity to mature as do wild dogs. They are forever dependent on us for food, water, access to the outdoors, and the like. It is not surprising that they become bossy. The problem digger must be changed from a bossy leader into a contented follower, at least to the point where it will stop digging.

Learn to Earn

Changing a bossy dog into one that accepts your wishes is easier to describe than to put into practice. The formula is simple: Each time your dog asks you to do something for it, you merely turn the tables and ask it to do something for you. Even if the request is only to Sit to gain approval or petting or dinner, you will thus be meeting two needs of the pet. A good follower *needs* to function for its leader. Your pet also *needs* your approval, which you express with praise and petting.

So, whenever you are approached for some attention, you must ask the dog to Sit or do something else. Then go ahead and praise and pet it, but only briefly. Avoid prolonged petting and fondling. Fondling spoils the program and the dog.

This aspect of your program is the single, most important one. It requires great self-control. Most of us have been well trained by our dogs to pet them whenever they want. We even do it without being conscious of it at times. However, it must be stopped to solve the problem.

When all of the previous steps are taken you will find a "new" dog in the house within a few days—a dog anxious to please, and more relaxed. Also you will be on your way to gaining a dog that begins to accept being left alone for longer and longer periods without digging.

If you have tied up your dog to keep it from digging, you should untether it. Too many animals have choked to death attempting to escape from tethers. Secure the yard as best you can if your pet is digging to escape.

Aids to Correction

A structural device that sometimes helps if the dog is digging out at a certain spot is a piece of plywood or sheet metal driven vertically, two feet into the ground. Allow at least four inches of the material above ground so the dog cannot dig into it and injure itself. The only shortcoming to this barrier is that some dogs may switch their digging to a different spot. However, if it is integrated with the entire program, this seldom occurs.

Dogs that dig in gardens or yards often are repelled by substances available commercially. If you have not tried any of these, they often help if used along with this program. Listerine mouthwash is distasteful to dogs, and can be sprayed on objects.

If you have been in the habit of taking the dog out for neighborhood walks, it is a good idea to curtail this during the program. When the problem is solved and six weeks have passed you can try a walk. If it produces backsliding, walks had best be abandoned.

Follow every step of the program that applies to your situation. Be patient and optimistic. Your pet will sense your mood and improve often more quickly than you imagine possible. The result should be a more responsive, better-adjusted dog.

Shyness — Kennelosis

A shy adult dog or puppy stirs strong emotions in people. These range from pity to embarrassment, but whichever it is, the problem usually troubles owners more than it does the pet. Nevertheless, shyness is a condition that can and should be dealt with immediately, or it may form the basis for other related problems.

UNDERSTANDING THE PROBLEM

To help dogs overcome shyness it is first necessary to understand how and why they become so. Dogs that are shy from early puppyhood very often live extremely isolated and sheltered lives with little contact with humans. They may in time become close only to one person and avoid all others. If allowed to mature in this situation they can replace shyness with downright hostility toward outsiders.

Wolves, coyotes and other wild members of the canine family are shy, but theirs is a self-preserving shyness. If they are born and raised in human homes and socialized with lots of people, they behave much like regular house pets. The deciding factor with shy dogs, domestic or wild, seems to be the slight amount of early human socialization they get. If your pet is in this category it will need much carefully supervised socialization to overcome the problem.

Learning Shyness

Some dogs learn shyness. That is, they have perhaps been frightened, overhandled or even unwittingly mishandled at some critical time in their lives. These dogs also need a socializing program, but often they require exposure only to the types of things that trigger the shy behavior.

Let us examine the signs of shyness your dog may display:
- Does it avoid all people, including you?
- If so, how does it behave when you approach or corner it?
- Does it snarl, freeze or wildly try to escape?

CORRECTING THE PROBLEM

To correct any type of shyness the principles are to build the dog's trust and then its self confidence. When these elements of your pet's personality develop, both of you will begin to enjoy life a great deal more. The program for overcoming shyness avoids all harshness, demands your patience and understanding, and is highly successful, even with dogs over four years old.

We can not force dogs to trust us. Trust is earned through consistent and considerate behavior. With your dog, you and others meeting it will need to behave in ways that remove all signs of threat, that invite the dog's approach, that build its trust and thereby allow its self-confidence to take root and grow.

Toward these goals, let us consider—from the dog's point of view—how to remove signs of threat.

Avoid "Fronting"

To animals bigness and face-to-face confrontation are threatening. The human voice may also signal a threat. If you stare, stand stock-still, smile or open your eyes extra wide, the dog may perceive any of these as a threat, even as a prelude to attack. Your position within a room or in relation to other people may also threaten a dog.

So, to avoid the possibility of threatening, set-ups need to be devised involving you and/or others of whom your pet may be shy. In the early stages of these set-ups, when the dog retreats or otherwise acts shy, here are the behavioral principles to follow:
- Position yourself about three feet away from the wall in the area, but stay within the dog's view.

- Stand sidewise to the dog, crouch, sit, or, in extreme cases, lie face down. (I will explain later about lying face down.)
- Try to occupy a position where the dog needs to pass by you to leave the area, but do not block its route.
- Move so as to cause the dog to have to approach you or others to escape the area.
- If the dog trusts some person, use that relationship to bridge trust from that person to one of whom the pet is shy.
- Hold sessions daily to build confidence.

CASE EXAMPLES

The best way to demonstrate these principles is by example.

A couple brought a handsome male Irish Setter to me. They had obtained the dog when it was seven months old from a breeding kennel. The dog took to the wife immediately, but it avoided the husband and all other people. The wife allowed the Setter to get up on the furniture beside her. When her husband or anyone else approached them the dog would get down and run into the closet in the couple's bedroom. Lately it had started growling at anyone approaching its hiding place.

The Irish Setter's condition is called kennelosis, which is common in dogs left in kennels beyond eight weeks of age before joining a human family. To demonstrate some of the principles for correction I asked the wife to sit on an outdoor couch while her husband and I sat down on chairs beside her. The Setter got up on her couch and lay down.

After I explained more of the program we all got up and walked side by side toward the gate that led to their car. The dog came along, but stayed at the wife's heels. We then turned around, returned to the seating area, and the wife and husband sat on the two chairs while I sat on the couch. The Irish Setter appeared confused by this switch, whined a little, and then tried to climb into the wife's lap. I told her not to be upset or scold him, merely to stand when he started to get up.

After about ten attempts to get on the lady's lap the dog jumped onto the couch, putting its head over as close to the wife as possible. After about five minutes we repeated the walk to the gate, but then the husband and I switched positions. The couple were amazed when their dog again got onto the couch.

The husband remarked, "This is the closest I have ever been to this dog!"

We got up again and returned, but this time both husband and wife sat on the couch so as to leave space for the Setter between them. Both of them beamed with surprised delight when the dog jumped up and actually licked the husband's hand before lying down. Needless to say, the ice had been broken and they were on their way to success.

Keep in mind that during this entire procedure we were paying no attention to the dog. No one said its name, made eye contact or faced it frontally. The pet was allowed the opportunity to make its own adjustments to the situation at its own pace. It took one hour, including our following discussion about how to make some set-ups when the couple returned home.

Another example is a dog who was shy, but loved to chase and fetch a ball. The same principles were applied, but the bridge between trusted people and others was the ball. It takes patience, but if the principles are applied, the plan becomes obvious and succeeds.

Extreme Case

If your dog is shy of everyone, even you, it may be necessary to take extreme measures to succeed. When you feed your pet, place the food dish between you and the dog. Then sit down about five feet from the dish with your back to it and the dog. Also, when you are home, take up the dog's water dish. When it is good and thirsty, fill the bowl and use this sit-down technique. If the dog will not approach food or water, try lying face down about six feet from the dish. One client of mine used this approach with success with an especially shy foundling dog who had evidently been abused.

These cases illustrate the principles allowing the dog to develop trust and build self-confidence at its own pace. If you will have patience in developing your program, and avoid trying to accomplish everything in a rush, you should see positive results after your very first set-ups with your pet. Give it up to six weeks to reach a point where you and your dog begin enjoying life with confidence.

Self-Mutilation

The dog that chews or licks itself severely enough to cause injury certainly starts doing it for some reason. At the outset, the reason is often physical but it can become a psychological-physical problem. For this reason, a correction program requires that you follow your veterinarian's advice to the letter. A let-down on the medical treatment may trigger irritation of the area involved and remind the pet to start chewing or licking again. By the same token it is necessary to adhere to the behavioral element or the physical condition can worsen.

MOTIVATIONS

Self-mutilation in dogs is quite different from the problem in people, in whom it has a self-destructive motivation. I have never heard of a dog consciously wanting to harm or destroy itself through this behavior. As a matter of fact, the opposite appears more likely. Wolves have been reported to chew off a foot in order to escape a leg-hold trap. The obvious goal is saving rather than destroying their lives.

So, the chances are good that your dog is chewing or licking itself, not neurotically, but to relieve some real irritation. At least it probably started out that way.

On the other hand, many dogs start to lick or chew themselves when left alone. Boredom can cause tension, a condition dogs can relieve through licking or chewing. Other dogs just do not accept being left alone. Thence the tension and the problem.

CORRECTING THE PROBLEM

Whatever may be causing the problem, the remedy is the same: give your pet something to do to relieve the tension. One of the most important facets of self-mutilation cases I find is that the dogs are not required on a consistent basis to earn their petting and praise. However, after our correction plan is in effect for a few days they begin to relax, become more responsive to their owners' directions and appear more contented. The way to achieve this is not difficult, but it requires self-control on everyone's part. More about this later on.

Use Play

Play is important in the lives of all dogs, both domestic and wild. People often forget this under the pressures of today's busy routines. So, one part of your program is to spend a few minutes a day, in the morning if possible, playing with your dog. Toss a ball or toy, run about the room or outside and let the pet chase you. Get its tail wagging! This intense, happy interaction is the type of activity that brings your dog out of itself and more in touch with you. Avoid playing tug-of-war, which can make the dog even more orally inclined when you leave it alone.

Defuse Emotion

Another element of your program is to defuse the emotions related to your comings and goings from home. This is not easy to do, but it will teach the dog that being left alone is not all that upsetting. This helps relieve the tensions that can result in self-mutilation. So, before leaving, spend a quiet five minutes or so in the area the dog will occupy when you are gone. Do not pay attention to the dog at all. Avoid even making eye-contact. Then get up and leave without so much as a word. This sets a quiet, relaxed example for the dog when you are away.

When you come home, say a friendly "Hi" and then go on about some other business for at least five minutes. When you do greet the dog, do so in an area away from the door by which you arrived. This helps relieve your pet's intense fixation on homecoming. The result is that the contrast in being with you or without you is lessened, making it easier to be alone.

After the self-mutilation has been cleared up for six weeks you may revert to warmer homecomings on arrival, but watch for backsliding. Curtail the welcomes if it happens.

Quid Pro Quo

Now for the most difficult part of the plan: To start your dog on its way to earning praise and petting, you must ask it to do something. Make it simple. Ask the dog to Sit, then say "Good Dog" as soon as it starts to sit, petting it when it sits down all the way. Make your petting quick, happy and brief—no more than about five seconds long.

Avoid fondling. More than any other action, fondling makes dogs introverted, and self-mutilation is a sign of introversion. Do not deny praise or petting, just be sure it is earned.

If the dog starts to pay attention to the mutilated area, instantly distract it with some sound or activity. Make the distraction sudden, like a slap on a table top or a quick movement toward another area. Avoid using your voice, or the correction will become dependent on your presence.

Conditioned Response

When you have applied a few corrections you should notice the dog start to look at the spot, lick or chew itself, but stop before you even have a chance to apply the correction. This is the conditioned response that will tend to be effective in your absence. Together with all other elements of the program, this conditioning is vital to success.

Continue every aspect of the program until the area of mutilation has remained clear for about six weeks. Then you may be sure the problem has been corrected. If you see any backsliding, simply reinstate the entire program for a few days.

If you and all who live with the pet follow the plan with optimism, you should start to notice results in a few days and a total correction in a few weeks.

Physical punishment is counter-productive.

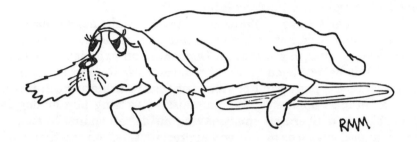

Wetting Submissively

When a puppy or mature dog starts wetting for no reason except that it is approaching or being approached by a person or another dog, or even when entering a certain area, the dog is not urinating deliberately. That is, it is not consciously performing the act but is responding on a purely emotional level. Something about the situation stimulates extreme feelings of submission in the dog.

So we can understand the dog's point of view in what seems like senseless behavior, let us examine where the act of submissive wetting originates.

FIRST SIGNS

The earliest submissive behavior puppies display is seen after their mother first feeds them. She nudges each pup over onto its back or side with her nose, holds it there and licks it from face to tail. The pup's reactions to this are to raise its paw when the mother is licking its chin and neck, which is where submissive paw-raising seems to originate. It then proceeds to urinate and defecate when the mother has licked its genitals and anus, which is where submissive urination has its roots.

225

As the pup grows older, gaining its eyesight, the mother merely has to look as if she intends to roll it over for the toilet ritual to achieve urination, if not defecation. This saves the mother time and also prepares the pups to become den-trained when they are able to follow outside for their eliminations later in life.

So, in its early stages, submissive urination is the puppy-response to a dominant look, but as the pups become more mature they gain some control over this response. Depending on experience, it may never again be displayed in adulthood. However, in cases of extreme stress (from the pup's point of view) submissive urination can recur.

One thing is apparent: Your submissive wetting pup or dog is probably not deliberately misbehaving but is responding to excitement, apprehension or fear. If you appreciate this, you can then deal with the problem without getting angry or upset. Submissive wetting demands well-controlled emotions if it is to be corrected.

ANALYZE THE PROBLEM

The problem usually occurs when the pet is faced by someone who approaches, takes a stance, looks or speaks threateningly or elicits excitement, such as at homecomings. Do a little fact-finding about your situation to determine when the wetting takes place:

- When you or others are facing the dog?
- When you lean over it?
- When reaching to pick it up?
- When you scold or raise your voice?
- When you or others get excited?
- At homecoming?

If you identify the things that trigger the dog's urination and are prepared to change your behavior, the problem can be cleared up. The time required will be from a few days to up to six weeks, depending on your skill and the severity of the problem.

CORRECTING THE PROBLEM

The first step is to remove any signs of threat at those key times when the dog wets: homecomings, visitors calling, when you scold the dog, etc.

If your pet wets when you approach, do not approach. Instead, crouch down and turn your side toward the dog. Do not hold out your hand, especially palm down or over the dog's head. Avoid direct eye contact. Let the dog approach you. If it seems to be under control, pet it under the chin, lightly. If this produces wetting, withhold petting for a few more days and then try it again.

Avoid Talking

Avoid speaking at these times for about four days. Then, see if saying "Good dog" will produce wetting. If not, keep up the routine for four days and on these occasions ask the dog to Sit and tell it "Good dog" when it complies. If speaking stimulates the wetting, withhold it for four days and then try it again.

Run through the situations at least three times in a row daily if you can. For instance, if entering at homecoming produces it, follow the program as just described, then go out and come in immediately again, and again.

In most situations four days are required before submissive wetting disappears when you remain crouched. When this happens you should approach the situation standing, keeping sideways to the dog.

If wetting occurs, go back into the crouch. Let the dog's reactions tell you how to behave. If you see that tell-tale squat begin, back off a step and start over until you can again proceed.

During the program your dog may gain so much confidence that it jumps up on you or others. Tolerate this for awhile, say about a week; then just sidestep, and the jumping will usually cease.

Involve Others

Avoid the mistake of carrying out the entire program yourself. Get others into the act. Make sure you let them know the techniques you are using. Show them. When several other people have gone through it with the dog, it will help make the correction permanent.

When two weeks have passed with none of the wetting, you can feel you have reached your goal. In case of backsliding, simply start at the beginning of the program again. Correction should only take a few sessions.

Throughout your program be patient, understanding and optimistic. Your mood will be sensed by your pet, and things will proceed more quickly.

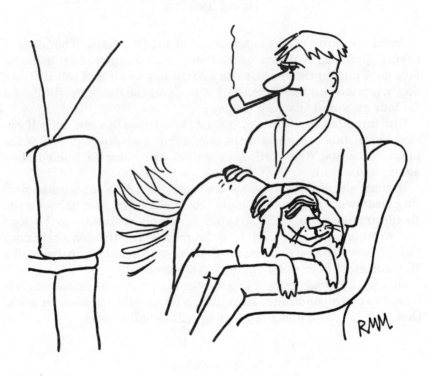

A dog should *earn* its petting.

"Can you give him something to relax his jaws?"

Aggression Toward Owners

This program deals with outright biting and emerging aggression shown by growling. Though the text uses the term "biting," you can substitute the word "growl" if your pet has not yet bitten, but appears on the verge of it.

The reasons for bites or growls may involve anything from overprotectiveness of food, toys and other articles, to a response to scolding or punishment. You can simply adapt the principles to your situation, since the same correction routine applies to all these problems.

When your own dog helps itself to some of your flesh, this is the ultimate insult. If ever I have heard a classic description of "ambivalence," it comes from bite victims.

"I wanted to kill that so-and-so, but I was shocked and my feelings were hurt to the quick," is the usual kind of statement. Also, most people say they aren't sure they can trust or feel the same warmth and affection for their pet ever again.

The meaning of the statement "Once bitten, twice shy" becomes painfully clear. It is extremely difficult to behave toward the dog with the same confidence as before. The dog senses this change and may take advantage of it, depending on the circumstances that led to the bite.

To start rehabilitating your relationship in a way that will also rebuild your confidence and allow you to correct the problem, you'll have to analyze what type of biting occurred.

REASONABLE vs UNREASONABLE BITING

All biting can probably be classified as defensive, in that it results from the dog's feeling threatened. For instance, if you were bitten while applying some physical punishment, it's simple to deduce that the biting was defensive. On the other hand, if you were merely telling the dog to get off the couch, using no threatening gestures, it is hard to say that the bite was defensive. However, in the couch situation, it was the dog's "status" (its feeling of dominance over you) that was threatened. In either case, the basic program for correction follows the same course.

We need to sort out "seemingly unreasonable biting" from "genuinely unreasonable biting." It is not unreasonable for a dog who feels it is the "boss" of its people to growl at or even bite its underlings if they fail to follow orders. This includes situations in which the human underlings want to pet the boss-dog. Extremely bossy dogs tell their people when and for how long they are permitted to pet them, not vice versa. Therefore, even though it may seem unreasonable, touching such a dog even affectionately when it is not in the mood threatens its dominant status.

This kind of dog, basically a leader, dominant and/or independent type, can be classified as "spoiled rotten." We'll call its biting "reasonable," at least to the dog!

The genuinely "unreasonable" biter is either out of its mind all the time or suffers episodes of seeming insanity. It might be better to say that people suffer from its brief episodes, since some of these dogs, after biting with apparently vicious intent, wag their tails, act submissively and literally lick the wounds they inflicted a few moments before, showing no signs of suffering at all.

These pets require a great deal more medical attention than their owners usually afford them. They should be given complete physical and neurologic examinations. If the dog is a purebred, the breeder should make a contribution to the cost, especially for a genetic chromosomal analysis.

In my experience, many unreasonable biters have suffered from arthritis, hip dysplasia, thyroid dysfunction (usually low), hormone imbalances, hydrocephalus (too much brain fluid pressure), cataracts, prediabetic and diabetic conditions, and even foxtails (grass awns)in the ears. If it is your fate to have such a dog, I hope you will consider medical examination as a reasonable approach to unreasonable behavior.

Some Cautions

If your biter has bitten an infant or child under the age of about six, but has not shown aggression to adults or other family children, your best bet is to follow the programs for Biting and for Children, New Pets and Dogs, which apply to such situations. This program is for family members old enough to understand its content and/or carry it out with parental supervision every step of the way.

Don't Punish

Physical punishment must be avoided if this program is to be effective. If your biter bit in reaction to physical punishment, this should seem obvious. On the other hand, if the dog was punished *after* some biting incident and biting is still a problem, the message must be the same: Do not use it.

The same holds true for "psychological" punishment, such as putting the dog outside. If this practice has not succeeded to date, it probably never will.

Don't Scold

This program assumes you have tried the "shame on you" and "bad dog" routines, with no improvement in the behavior problem. So, scolding must also be avoided.

The Hyperkinetic Biter

Hyperkinetic dogs, like their child counterparts, are constantly on the move, always seeking attention. They are four-legged response-mechanisms looking for a stimulus. I have even seen them bump into chairs, just to get the feedback of the chair's movement! When hyperkinetics also bite, they are usually deemed "psychotic," because their total behavior seems unreasonable.

Physically they may appear normal, but most of those I have met have slightly enlarged pupils, even on bright, sunny days. Compared to normal dogs, they drink very litle water. When held in mild restraint their heart and breathing rates go sky high. Some of them salivate a great deal, but they usually swallow their saliva.

It is important not to confuse a hyperexcitable dog with a genuine hyperkinetic. Hyperexcitable dogs overreact to activities around them. Hyperkinetics do not need activities around them; they are always on the move, making things happen around them.

Many hyperkinetics outgrow their condition. If this has happened to your dog, do not use it for breeding. The condition could be passed on to offspring.

Many hyperkinetics respond well to medication that would make a normal dog (or child) hyperactive. Instead, the genuine hyperkinetic calms down dramatically and appears to become normal. Often the hyperkinetic biter ceases to show any hostile behavior. If this occurs, the dog can be worked through a program of biting correction and responds even more positively than the nonhyperkinetic biter.

Both the medical and behavioral programs for correction in these cases need veterinary supervision and guidance. However, they are well worth the time and effort required.

CORRECTION OF BITING

Social Distance

To change your relationship with your biting dog, you must put some "social distance" between you and it. This does not mean physical distance. Rather, it means that interactions between you should be unemotional. To acomplish this, all you need to do is take care of the dog's physical needs. This should involve the following, and no more:

- Feed it on a twice-a-day schedule.
- Keep its water bowl full.
- Let it outside or take it out for toilet duties only. If you have been taking it for walks, suspend them until later in the program.
- Avoid all eye contact with the dog.
- Do not speak to the dog, except when absolutely necessary.
- Avoid physical contact with it, except as required for its well-being. For instance, if the dog comes over and leans on you, or gets onto the furniture, merely move away in a neutral manner.

These steps avoid emotional interchange between you and the dog, and set the stage for a revised relationship. This shows itself in many ways. The dog may increasingly try to get your attention, or it may even "pout" for a couple of days. If it tries the pouting routine, let it and wait until it starts soliciting your attention for petting or praise.

This cooling-off period allows you to assess your own feelings about both the biting incident and the dog. When you feel the dog is trying to warm up to you, and when you feel confident in renewing your emotional and physical relationship (petting, not punishing), the time is usually right to start reestablishing a proper social standing with your pet—one in which you are the leader. This usually takes two to four days.

Determining the Problem

Getting bitten by your own dog usually happens because of some other behavior problem. If this is the case, consult the appropriate problem-program: Chewing, Jumping, Barking, etc. and follow that program in conjunction with this one.

Earning Leadership

If you are to be seen by your pet as its leader, you must function as a leader. Tell the dog to do something, such as "Tippy, Sit," each time it asks for your attention and/or petting. If the dog is already sitting, tell it to Lie Down. Briefly praise and pet happily for obedience. Do not ask it to sit for dinner or breakfast or tidbits of food. You want the dog functioning for *you,* not for food. Besides, "the hand that feeds" has already been bitten!

When You've Got "IT"

"IT" is a sense of having control over your dog's feelings, as well as its behavior. You can tell by the dog's reactions to your praise, after it responds to Sit or Down.

You won't have "IT" if, instead of sitting, the dog starts jumping on you or goes away, barks or pouts, which may happen with extremely bossy dogs.

You will have "IT" when you see your pet's emotional energy and attention directed to what you want, rather than what it wants.

When you feel you have this control, you can start the correction program for another behavior problem, if there was one that led to the biting in the first place.

Approaching the Biting Situation

If you were bitten in such a situation as when telling the dog to get off the furniture or while handling it, you need to understand that it bit to put you in your "underling" place. You must now summon all the sense of humor you possess. This "Jolly Routine" also applies if the dog bit you when, due to poor lighting, it seemed not to recognize you.

You must create or be vigilant to take advantage of that certain situation, should it be one that is difficult to arrange, such as coming home and finding the dog on the furniture.

Apply the Jolly Routine

The instant the dog notices you and is in the situation, clap your hands and say whatever makes the dog wag its tail. You know what phrases "turn on" your dog, so use them. Some examples are:

- "Good dog, Tippy. Let's get the ball!"
- "Good dog, Tippy. Wanna go out?"

As you say the good-time phrase, move away from the dog and toward the ball, the door, etc. Get the dog to follow you. Do not approach the dog. If it follows, play with the ball, or follow through on the activity that started the routine.

If it is a semidarkness biting situation, follow the jolly-phrase by turning on adequate light as you move away and attract the dog out of the situation.

If possible, go through the Jolly Routine a couple of times a day, but do not try to repeat it more than twice in a single situation. Its impact can be diluted if it is overdone. Besides, the new emotional reactions need time to incubate if they are to be retained by the dog.

Remember: Never create a situation or go into a session unless you feel you have control over the dog's mood. If you feel shaky, your heart is in your mouth or your pulse is pounding, return to the Earning Leadership phase until you have settled down and feel confident again. Also keep in mind that, with an extremely bossy dog, you must make leadership the hallmark of your lifelong relationship.

If you follow the principles involved in the cooling-off period, and the leadership and jolly phases with confidence, you should be back on an even keel with your dog after six weeks or so.

In the event you do not seem to be getting anywhere with this program, you could benefit from the services of an experienced dog behavior consultant.

Unruliness

Frustration, embarrassment and more frustration: These are the emotions we dog owners can feel when a pet continually dashes outdoors, or "sexes" visitors by sniffing them in private places. The dog that is just plain overactive, especially when guests arrive, can also be helped toward better behavior with this program. Correction for all these conditions starts with the same step—establishing yourself and other household members as leaders and teachers for the pet.

LEARNING TO EARN ATTENTION

If a dog learns it must do something to earn its praise and petting, it soon learns to look to you for guidance in all of life's situations. It is not necessary to break a pet's spirit through punishment or scolding, to gain control. Rather, consistency and good-natured perseverance are effective and humane. Your understanding and use of the dog's natural language—body movement and stance—also are necessary to leadership. The following steps are for all household members.

Each time your dog asks for attention, ask it to Sit. The technique does not require heavy handling. You merely keep your left side toward the dog, lean slightly backward, and bring your right hand through its line of vision to a point above the animal's head. This causes the dog to look upward and back, tracking your hand. Raising its head is the first part of sitting for dogs, so say "Good sit" when it happens. Keep up this procedure until the dog actually sits. Then praise more and pet it, preferably on the throat and chest. After a few sessions of this, over two to four days, the dog should be sitting readily on your spoken "Sit", or even with the hand movement alone.

Be sure everyone follows this routine with your pet. Use it whenever you want to pet it, and when the dog wants some of your attention.

Some bossy dogs may "pout" when they realize you are turning the tables on them, that is, asking them to earn their praise and taking a position of leadership with them. Such pouting may include going away from you rather than sitting for you. If this happens, simply go on about your business and ignore it. Pouting is great self-therapy for bossy dogs. You will notice that the pet's need for attention overcomes the bossiness, and it will return to Sit for praise. This may take up to four days with extremely bossy dogs. It is well worth it, though, since the problems to be worked out will require your leadership.

DASHING OUTDOORS

Many people like to use the Sit to stop a dog from dashing through a door. The trouble with this is two-fold:

- If you forget to ask for the Sit, the dog dashes.
- The dog never develops self-control about dashing.

The goal of this method, and it is extremely effective, is to instill self-control over door-dashing in your dog. When this is achieved, a genuine correction has been gained. Therefore, movement and body language will speak more clearly than Sit, since these are the natural channels of canine communication.

Learning to use movement with your dog requires that you react quickly to the pet. This means you must keep an eye on the dog at all times, being ready to reverse your direction the instant the dog starts to move the wrong way. Here is how it works at the door.

Start to move toward the door through which the dog likes to dash. This might be any door in the house, or only the front door. As you start toward the door, if the dog appears about to go toward it, abruptly back away from the door, praising the dog, even crouching down to attract it away from the portal. Repeat this until you can approach the door while your dog stays away from it. At this point return quickly to your dog and praise it again. During this part of the program, make the area to which you back up at least five feet from the door.

Phase two involves starting to open the door. As you do so, watch the dog! If it starts to break toward you, repeat the abrupt back-away routine. If you got the door open before your pet's movement toward you, slam the door before backing away for the praise. Repeat this until you can open the door with the dog remaining away. Then, once again, close the door and go back and praise the dog.

Phase three requires you to go through the door, keeping your eye on the dog, and close it. Stay outside for about thirty seconds. Then go inside to the spot away from the door and praise your dog. At this point you may have to start over at phase one because your dog tends to learn by phases before it can learn the entire procedure as a single process. However, if you will keep repeating the process, the dog will learn it within a few minutes.

Practice this routine on all doors and with all household members. Do it in groups of people as well. Do it with packages in your arms and in all of the situations the dog will encounter in life at the door.

Another interesting technique that works well with dogs that dash merely to be with people is to let the animal go out through the door, (into an area safe from any harm, of course). Close the door and leave the dog on the other side. Then open the door and let the pet in or out, as the case may be. Do this a few times and the dog soon will look to you before dashing. However, you must then revert to phase one for long-term correction.

EMBARRASSING SNIFFING-LICKING

It does not require elaborate description to communicate the embarrassment of an owner or the chagrin of a victim when a dog nuzzles the private area of a guest. Even other dogs seem to object to such intrusions. The offending pet, obeying basic and primitive drives, may be curious as to the sex of visitors, but must learn better manners for its own and the owner's long-range well being. If your pet is among the oversniffers, or licks people to excess, this program is simple and effective.

Remove the Cause

The dog that learns to Sit for its introduction to guests is not only well-mannered but unoffensive. That is to say, people who may be wary of meeting new dogs seem reassured by a sitting dog. Therefore, teach your pet to Sit and to stay sitting until you release it with the word "Okay." Gradually increase the sitting time from ten seconds to two minutes.

When greeting guests, have the pet sit and then allow the newcomers to say hello, offering a hand, palm up, for the dog to sniff. In the event your visitors are confident with dogs, have them crouch down so the pet can scent their breath. To many mammals the essence of our being, in terms of identification, seems to be embodied in our breath. Once they have sampled it, they usually are satisfied and further curiosity is quelled.

Following the hand- and breath-sniff routine, have the guests be seated and release the dog. It may proceed to make the rounds, saying another "hello" and then should calm down.

If the foregoing program is put into effect for a few visits, you should notice your pet sitting automatically when greeting newcomers. This is a goal achieved by more than half of the dogs put through this program. If your guests will be staying for longer than an evening, it is best to have them ask the dog to sit for them, then pet, then release the dog. This places the guests in a position of control and has proven positive in controlling the sniffer-licker. The entire routine seems to satisfy the pet's basic desire to identify by scent, and the tendency to be curious about parts of the anatomy usually fades in two to six weeks.

The foregoing program should be applied in the very same way for dogs who get overexcited and hyperactive when guests arrive. If it is applied persistently and consistently, the result can be a well-mannered dog who will be welcome in the house with your guests.

Swallowing Non-Foods

If your dog swallows things that have no nutritional value, it has a condition called pica. Pica is sometimes seen in pregnant women and people with intestinal parasites or a certain iron deficiency. These are also causes in dogs, and your veterinarian is the only person qualified to diagnose them. If your pet is on a program of medication, follow the doctor's directions to the letter, or the behavioral phase of your program will suffer.

FORCE OF HABIT

Certain factors seem to be common in cases of pica. You may find one or more of these in your pet's background:
- The dog has been extremely oral from puppyhood.
- It will chew on itself when deprived of other articles.
- When the problem began, people would pull things from its mouth.
- The dog enjoys a game of tug-of-war.

Although these elements are found in some dogs that do not suffer from pica, they appear with consistency in those that do have problems.

239

Once pica becomes a habit, major problems can result. If your pet is so affected and has not required surgery to remove something it has swallowed, consider yourself lucky.

Some of the psychologic forces at work in the condition need consideration in order to understand the correction methods.

Puppies, just like human offspring, seem to want to put everything new in their mouths. Pups usually decide the article is good to chew or they reject it. Swallowing it is probably the last thing in their plan at this stage. When people pull the article out of the pup's mouth before a decision can be made, some animals develop a stronger desire for it. Also, the puppy may learn that taking such things in its mouth brings attention, even if negative, and so carry on the practice.

Food Reinforcement

When a pup finally swallows something that may be harmful, it is often fed bread or cake to ease the thing through its intestines. Another positive reinforcement has thus been given: food. The better alternative is to call the veterinarian immediately.

Feeding only once a day leaves a dog with an empty stomach for up to 19 hours out of each 24, which invites pica. So it is a requirement of this program to feed at least twice daily.

Symbolic Pica

A most common element in pica is the eating of articles that belong to or symbolize the owner. This usually occurs when the dog is left alone, or when the owner merely takes his or her attention off the pet while at home. It is as if the dog were using pica to gain attention, even in the form of punishment.

BREAKING THE HABIT

From all these causes for pica, you may recognize an element or two common to your situation. Even if not, the following program has solved hundreds of cases and should benefit your dog, if followed strictly.

Earning Attention

Most dogs with pica miss their owners too much when left alone or ignored. They strive for all the attention they can get. To make your pet more contented you will now have to ask that it earn its petting and praise. So, each time your dog begs, or you want to give it attention, ask it to Sit for you. If it is sitting already, ask it to Lie down. In other words, get it to function for you.

It is amazing to see dogs settle down and become more relaxed after a few days of this little routine.

Avoid prolonged petting; make it only about five seconds. Fondling dogs tends to make them introverted, and pica is a sign of introversion.

Tone Down Emotions

To help your dog stop missing you too much, it will be necessary to defuse the emotions involved in your comings and goings from the house.

Before leaving home, take just five minutes and sit down in the area the dog will occupy in your absence. Ignore the dog, read a paper or just gather your thoughts about the day's activities. This sets a calm, unconcerned prelude to the departure. Do not even make eye contact with the dog. Then get up and leave without any words or ceremony.

At homecoming say "Hi" and then go about doing some other business for five minutes. Then you may ask the dog to Sit and give it a nice "hello." However, do this in an area away from the door by which you entered. This avoids too much emotion in the area of your homecoming.

All of these steps help eliminate the causes for the tensions that result in pica. When we get rid of the causes by getting the pet to function for praise and petting, and relieve the emotional uproar about homecomings and goings, the dog should become noticeably more relaxed within a few days or weeks.

After the Fact

What should you do if you come home and the dog has swallowed something? It is too late to take remedial action. The dog has long since forgotten the act of swallowing the article. However, if you think something harmful has been swallowed, call your veterinarian without delay.

When you are home and the dog shows interest in something it may swallow or if it even mouths or chews, distract it instantly. Clap your hands, or slap a wall with your hand or a newspaper. Do not slap the dog or speak to it, because we want to depersonalize the correction so it will be effective even when you are not at home. Then, toss a ball or some acceptable chewy toy to provide a substitute for the forbidden article.

Never pick up things you do not want your pet to have while the dog is watching you. You can actually heighten the desire for it. Dogs seem to enjoy "handling" with their mouths the things we handle.

Play Relaxes

The final element of the program is play. This is especially important if your pet is alone a great deal. Toss a ball, run around and let the dog chase you, at least once a day. Do it in the morning if you can. This helps give proper exercise and also provides an intense, happy emotional interaction that relaxes the dog.

Continue the program at least six weeks. You will not be spending any extra time, only changing the way you are spending time with your pet. If your dog is on medical treatment during the program, follow your veterinarian's advice strictly. Total correction of any behavior problem depends on the physical well-being of the dog as well as its emotional health.

The largest sacrifice you will make is emotional—giving up those joyous homecoming celebrations and fondling. However, pica is a serious problem, and the ultimate good for you and your pet is well worth the effort.

Sympathy Lameness

Nothing is more pitiful than an injured animal, especially a puppy. When it is our own pet, the effect on us can be more upsetting than the injury is to the animal. Sympathy Lameness is a condition that occurs long after the animal's injury has healed. A full understanding of the cause brings about the insights needed for a correction.

REFLEXIVE PAW-RAISING

When puppies or older dogs feel concerned about some of life's situations, they often lift one of their forepaws. Some even whine. This behavior stems from early experience with their canine mothers who, after feeding them, nuzzled them over onto their backs and commenced to lick them, first around the muzzle and neck, then down their abdomen and across their genitals and anus. This stimulated their primary reflex to eliminate (urinate and defecate) which is thus a learned reflex in puppies, not a natural reflex as in human and primate infants. During the licking, especially around their muzzles, the still-sightless pups raise their forepaws in an effort to ward off this post-feeding maternal "treatment." The result of all this is that paw-raising is associated with objection to being dominated.

When puppies graduate into the human family, you will often see this behavior come with them. If you roll a pup onto its back and gently hold it immobile, you can usually see the paws start rising immediately. If you hold it thus for thirty seconds or so, you can even judge just how submissive or dominant the pup feels; if it calms down quickly and becomes still, it is fairly submissive; if it struggles fiercely the entire time, it feels fairly or extremely dominant. Submissive pups often raise their paws or even roll onto their backs when scolded. Dominant types often put their paws onto the arms of a person who tries to pet them on the throat and chest.

If you get the idea that submissive types are more prone to sympathy lameness than dominant types, you are on the right track. But it does not always hold true, especially if the lameness starts following a painful experience.

ACQUIRED SYMPATHY LAMENESS

There are several ways to cause sympathy lameness. One of the less common is to deliberately teach it. Every time the pup or dog raises its paw, give it a reward, such as sympathetic attention to that paw. Soon each time the pet wants some attention, it will raise the paw.

Accidentally causing the condition is more common and usually follows some incident such as stepping on the paw. This brings about the familiar yip, followed by apologies and cuddling by the remorseful pain-inflictor. The pain of the accident was real, but the emotional interpretation of it may be even more vivid to the dog. That is, the apologetic person is telling the pup that this experience is horrible, and warrants a great deal of attention and sympathy. Depending on the sensitivity of the puppy, the degree of pain, and the intensity of the sympathy offered, sympathy lameness may occur later in several circumstances:

- When the puppy or dog wants attention.
- When the owner uses a sympathetic tone of voice.
- When the paw or limb is handled with concern.

The latter two reasons are easy to relate to the problem. However, the first reason pops up in rather baffling ways.

Case Example

An unusual case involved a spayed Doberman that had received extreme sympathy as a puppy when she suffered what appeared to be a mild seizure. Thereafter, whenever visitors arrived and her owner's attentions were directed elsewhere, she became hostile toward the guests. On the other hand, when family members gathered to play games, the Doberman would often fall on her side and have another seizure. This interrupted the games, of course, and led to the attention she had learned to attain through what is called pseudoepilepsy.

Another dog may not have a general seizure, but the tell-tale paw will rise or limping will start in the affected limb.

Many of my cases have involved sympathy lameness in the following situations:

- A new baby arrives home.
- A new pet is introduced into the home.
- One of the family goes away for some time.
- An argument occurs in the home.
- There is a general undertone of stress in the emotional environment, eg, someone is ill or upset and the dog, in its uncanny way, senses it.

Our pets are incredibly sensitive to our emotions, even when we try to hide them. Therefore, since "feelings" are the key to causing sympathy lameness, they are also the tools for correcting the problem.

CORRECTING THE PROBLEM

There are two ways to correct sympathy lameness. The first is often the easiest: Avoid the things that bring on the problem. This is simple to do if it only occurs when you use a concerned tone of voice, or scold or punish your pet. However, when the various triggers for the lameness are not controllable, a different routine must be used. The dog must be taken through the situations that cause lameness, and then you must show it a different interpretation and a new way to behave rather than becoming lame.

The Jolly Routine

Whenever your dog shows signs of becoming lame, you must start an upbeat, happy activity for everyone, especially the pet. This might be bouncing a ball, running about and tossing a favorite toy, getting the leash and suggesting a quick walk—the Jolly Routine.

The routine must be started before the actual lameness sets in and should last about three minutes or longer. Then return to whatever activity started the signs of lameness, again switching to the Jolly Routine if there is the slightest sign that the dog is going to act lame again. Repeat the routine until your pet no longer responds with lameness. Undertake this procedure daily if possible, but at least three times weekly until, when you start the activity that formerly produced lameness, you now see the dog get active. When this point is attained, you no longer need to go into your Jolly Routine. However, watch for backsliding. Depending on the age of your pet, it might occur. If it does, restart the routine and cease when the correction is effective.

At first, you and others in the household may feel a little silly, jumping about joyfully when the dog is asking for sympathy, but switching the pet's mood of concern to one of happy activity will work wonders if you are all sincere and stick to the program.

"You can bring Fury in now, Mrs. Caslick."

Overprotectiveness

If your adult dog or pup has shown signs of overprotectiveness, consider yourself fortunate if it has not yet bitten anyone. Many dog owners who see the first signs of protecting in their pets later fail to recognize the danger when overprotectiveness emerges. As a matter of fact, some people feel good and even encourage the behavior until a bite occurs.

CAUSES OF THE PROBLEM

To correct the problem let us first look at the causes. Overprotection results from a combination of the dog's built-in capabilities to protect members of its group, whether human or canine, and the actions of the group members themselves. In other words, the way you and other family members have reacted to your dog's first signs of protectiveness may have contributed to the problem.

In today's society it is quite normal to feel insecure to some degree. Radio, TV and the newspapers pummel our senses with a great deal of violence. Then, when a stranger approaches our door and our dog shows early signs of protecting us, we may feel somehow reassured. It is uncanny the way dogs seem able to sense our emotional reactions to such situations. And these emotions often reinforce the dog's aggressiveness. In this way we can unwittingly contribute to the problem.

247

In other cases family members deliberately praise the behavior, even urging the pet to menace outsiders. We see this most often when children are involved.

Owner Insecurity

Another unwitting contributor to the problem is the owner who secretly feels insecure and allows the dog to take the role of leadership. In any relationship a dog has with people or other dogs, one or the other is going to be leader. When the dog is allowed to assume this role it often tends to overdo its territorial and group protectiveness.

As you may have gathered, it takes a bit of soul-searching on the owner's part to find the role he or she may play in an overprotection problem. It also requires carefully controlled emotions and strict adherence to this program to achieve success in molding the overprotective dog into a dependable pet that will properly protect its people.

Bossy Signs

Consider seriously your relationship with your dog: What goes on in daily life with it?

- When you leave home, does the dog try to beat you out the door?
- If you go to another room and close the door, does the dog get upset?
- When you embrace someone, are there any signs of jealousy?
- Does your dog seem to demand a great deal of petting? And do you respond by giving it what it wants?
- Would you be disappointed if your pet showed some other person preference over you?

If your dog is overprotective about you, and if you answer some of these questions "yes," you may be starting to appreciate your part in the problem. Furthermore, the chances are that you are not at fault. It is normal for a dog owner to feel emotionally comforted by the pet's affection. The problem is whether the dog or the owner is *directing* the occasions and duration of displays of affection.

Petting Must be Earned

If the dog gets petted every time it desires, it is natural that it may begin to object if other people come around and interrupt this activity. If it shows its objections with overprotectiveness, and the owner either scolds or tries to reassure it, the problem usually becomes more serious.

In other words, the pet is not really protecting its people, but protecting its selfish relationship with them, ie, its "right" to have its own way with them.

If the pet is punished physically or put away when visitors arrive, it can quickly learn to hate the sight and sound of all future visitors.

So much for the various causes of the problem. The important thing now is to enter into its correction with an enlightened attitude, avoiding things that played a part in the problem's development.

CORRECTION BY SOCIALIZING

An overprotective dog requires a program of broad socialization with lots of different people. Furthermore, it needs you, its leader, to show it how to behave in order to build its confidence about people. *The pet that does not feel confident about people cannot learn to recognize those with unfriendly intentions.* Such a dog may be fine for military guarding work, but is dangerous as a family pet. So, take your dog out to meet people, show it how to feel and behave by acting friendly *yourself* with those whom you know and trust.

When you first meet people, try to stand alongside of them and chat for awhile. Do not face them. Face-to-face, in the dog's view, signals a confrontation. When you are at a person's side the pet perceives you as friendly with that person.

If you take your dog out on a leash, make sure you do not allow it to strain when you meet people. Holding a dog back by a leash from other people is a technique used in training attack dogs.

If you have a dog with hair that hangs over its eyes, do your pet a favor and tie it up or, better yet, cut it off. As mentioned elsewhere, life down on the floor is tough enough without having to look at the world through a picket fence. This will avoid visual surprise when people reach to pet or pick up the dog. Contrary to a popular myth, "hairy-eyed" dogs do not go blind when their eyes are exposed to sunlight.

Gain Confidence

If you do not feel confident of your ability to control your dog on a leash, find a humane, competent trainer who will teach you how to handle the leash. Avoid trainers that want to take your dog by the leash and train it for you. Such treatment only makes you seem less competent with the leash by comparison with an expert.

Along with your program of socialization, general environmental adjustments are required. In most cases of overprotection, the dogs have pretty well trained their people to pet them whenever the dogs want it. The dogs stimulate and the people respond. The leaders say "Pet me," and their subjects obey!

Pet Wisely

The worst thing I could advise you to do is to stop petting your dog. But do turn around the stimulus-response pattern of the relationship. When your dog approaches to ask for some affection and petting, you now merely ask it to Sit and then go ahead and pet it, making the petting brief and happy. Avoid excessive fondling, which tends to spoil the dog and will ruin your program.

After a few days of this treatment your dog will begin to realize it must function by following your lead, to gain the social gratification it needs. This is good. You may also find the dog more willing to please you in other of life's situations. It will tend to be less competitive going through doors, more content and relaxed.

In the early stages of this routine the dog may resist sitting for you and go away. If this happens, just ignore it. Pouting is great self-therapy, and the dog will come around in two to four days. Do not feel rejected. Just wait it out and you will gain your position of leadership.

Use Toys

A final note about your socializing program—if your dog likes to play fetch or chase a ball, use this device with people who come to visit, at the park and in all the situations where overprotection has been evident. Give the ball to other people and let them toss it to help strengthen the dog's confidence. Act jolly and confident yourself, and you will set the best example for your dog.

On the other hand, if you do not feel confident, avoid having the session of socialization. Otherwise you will transmit your feelings to the pet and your work will be counterproductive. Wait until another day when you feel better about it.

Follow this program and at the end of six weeks you should have a dog that is confident, friendly and still able to protect if and when the need genuinely arises.

Fighting Dogs

When dogs fight, the primitive savagery horrifies any mentally healthy dog owner. Some unbalanced people actually promote dog fights, betting on the outcome. These sadists and masochists use their dogs as extensions for their compulsions to hurt or to be hurt. However, even normal dog owners can unwittingly promote dog fights.

CAUSES

"My dog can lick your dog" is an attitude lurking below the surface in many dog owners, especially children. Also when a stray dog is shooed away angrily in the family dog's presence, this can overstimulate the family dog's feelings about territorial protection and promote fighting.

Another cause for fighting is an attack by another dog. Often the victim thereafter reacts with extreme aggression to all other dogs.

Two or more dogs in the same household may start fighting as they mature, especially if they are littermates or the same sex.

Serious fighting in family dogs usually has its roots in the way people react to the first early signs of threat displays between the pets. If you will recall these early scuffles, you can probably answer the following questions affirmatively:

251

• Were the dogs pulled apart?

• Was one or both of the dogs punished or angrily scolded?

These reactions, though quite normal, can actually heighten hostility between the pets. Such human actions do not necessarily get across the right message to the dogs.

When we interfere, the dogs think we are joining the fray! If one dog is punished, the other one may feel we are taking its side. This can make that dog "punish" the other at a later time. Even simple scolding can create this reaction.

After years of consulting with the owners of fighting dogs, my records show it was the owners who escalated the early threat displays into full-blown battles. On the positive side of the record, however, the same owners corrected the problem by following a program to intervene in a different way with their pets.

It usually takes six weeks to correct the problem. But, if your dogs have punctured each other or have fought five or more times, more time may be required to gain peace and contentment.

WILD DOGS

Before outlining the correction program it will help to consider dogs in their natural social situation, living with a pack of dogs rather than with people. In the wild, every dog has a function—a job. Hunting is a highly organized matter, and survival of the pack requires each animal to perform its function successfully. Injury or death of any member endangers the total pack welfare.

Peace and the pecking order are maintained through displays rather than serious fighting. These displays are rituals in which a dominant dog menaces an underling, who responds submissively by either lowering its head, perhaps snarling as a seeming objection, rolling onto its side or back, urinating, or even running away with its tail down. Seldom does any physical injury occur, and the ritual maintains harmony.

Many of these behaviors may also be seen in litters of domestic puppies. They do not persist, however, because the pups are soon placed in human homes.

DOMESTICATED DOGS

You may be wondering at this point if it is going to be necessary to change your home into one resembling a pack of dogs in order to correct warring dogs. No. I have found it far easier and more effective to "humanize" dogs than to "uncivilize" people. However, the success of the program depends on you and others around the dogs. You must establish a strong leadership position with them and dominate the emotional climate of the environment. A goodly amount of self-discipline is required, but success can be achieved if the program is followed strictly.

The first step is to have faith in the dog's incredible ability to adapt —to change its feelings and behavior in response to changes in the environment.

In the early stages of the program you may want to keep your fighting dog or dogs separated from the adversary. Also, if your dogs fight when left alone they must be kept separated. When we cannot control the stimulus for fighting, it would be inhumane to leave the dogs to their own fate.

Show Leadership

The first change required is to demonstrate to the pet that its people are good-natured, consistent, competent leaders. Dogs with this type of leadership seldom vie for dominance or fight.

To reach this leadership goal every person in the household must ask the dog(s) to do something to earn praise or petting. This should be something simple, such as Sit, or some other thing the dog does well. This must be done each time the dog asks for attention or when people want to give it attention.

Do not order your dog to act; just ask pleasantly, then praise it when it starts to obey and pet it when it completes the act. Make your petting quick, happy and brief—no longer than three to five seconds.

Avoid absent-minded stroking, or fondling. It can create jealousies and ruin your program. When about four days of this treatment have gone by you should begin to see a more responsive pet, more willing to accept direction. When this happens you are ready to go on to the next step.

Jollity Pays

Every dog has something that makes it happy. It may be a bouncing ball or some other toy, hearing "Good Dog" and happy-acting people, or a suggestion of a car ride. Whatever device turns on the happy switch with your pet, use it as the key part of what I call the Jolly Routine. This routine is used to switch the dogs from hostile to happy moods when they first come together.

The exposure of the dogs to each other can be through glass doors, a fence, on leashes or in a free situation. You must choose how to do it, based on your ability to control the dogs and the mood of the set-up.

The very *instant* the dogs become aware of each other, the Jolly Routine must be started. Bounce the ball, say "Good Dogs," and get the tail-wagging response. Then take them away from each other, or leave them together if they seem peaceful. If they are left together, be vigilant and ready to start the jolly business again if you see any signs of impending trouble, such as stiffness of gait, staring or a tail raised high. If so, get jolly again!

Follow this routine twice daily if possible. Continue it until you see the dogs start to wag their tails even *before* you can apply the Jolly Routine.

At that time a valuable goal has been reached, a genuine conditioned switch in mood from hostility to jollity.

Carry on the program for at least six weeks to gain virtually permanent correction. Longer programs are required in more severe cases.

Away from Home

If you feel your home territory is part of the cause for fights, take the dogs to another place for the early set-ups. In any case, be sure to distract them with the Jolly Routine if either starts to urinate. The act of urinating seems a bit like muscle-flexing in people— challenging.

If your dog fights other dogs in the neighborhood, do not allow it to urinate outside your own backyard. Otherwise you will be allowing it to extend its territory beyond the boundaries of its own property, which invites fighting.

Always keep in mind the program's principles:
 • Gain strong leadership for all family members.
 • Ask the dog(s) to earn praise and petting.
 • Stop all fondling of the pets.
 • Use the Jolly Routine during your formal sessions and if any sign of hostility appears.

Conduct the program in circumstances that you can control, apply good-natured determination, and persevere for at least six weeks. If this is done you should achieve peace and tranquility.

Killing Animals

If your dog has killed other animals, you are faced with one of the most difficult problems. Basically, three types of animal killers are found, and the types are defined according to the dog's emotional state during the attack. They are:

- Angry killers
- Playful killers
- Predatory, cold-blooded killers

If your dog kills in anger, a complete program can be found for it in the program on Fighting, and that program should be instituted immediately and followed faithfully.

PLAYFUL vs PREDATORY KILLERS

Playful types usually target on birds, gophers, fowl and other small mammals. This program will deal with that problem.

Predatory, cold-blooded types are the most difficult to rehabilitate and require extreme dedication to succeed. Most predatory types do not eat their prey; it is only their approach to killing that is predatory. Deliberate stalking, lying in wait, attacking the target animal at the base of the neck (a predator kill area) are the hallmarks of these dogs.

Their entire procedure can be bone-chilling to witness, since their prey are totally unaware of their intentions until too late.

Most animal killers in my case files have a history of too little activity with their owners. This is often coupled with a history of being "sicced" by the owners on stray animals that entered their territory. Even the innocent act of shooing animals away from the property can be interpreted by some dogs as a license to attack and kill. If this has been your unwitting error, you will now need to reverse your course and appear happy when intruders appear.

STEPS TO REHABILITATION

Most animal-killing dogs are leader-types. That is, they tend to be bossy in their relationships with their family members, or are loners. In either case, the dogs must learn that you and others in the household are going to teach them. This is more difficult with loners, since they do not show as much need for attention as do others. However, this program has succeeded nicely, even with some highly independent types.

The first step is to gain a strong orientation toward yourself, in order to establish your leadership role with the dog. It requires that you ignore your pet completely, except to feed it, supervise its toilet activities and whatever other activities are absolute necessities, such as opening doors. You must cut off all play and petting, and even avoid eye-contact, until the point is reached where the dog appears frustrated and in dire need of attention or approval. With some independent types, this ignore-the-dog routine may require up to four days before the desired orientation is gained. At this point you can proceed to the second step.

Step two requires that you now show your pet affection, but only after it has responded to some direction from you. This direction can be as simple as asking it to Sit or Lie Down. Then you should pet it briskly with upbeat praise for no longer than about five seconds. Avoid all soft, prolonged petting or fondling. If your dog does not perform a sit for you, teach it.

Teaching Sit requires first that you teach Come. This is important in this program. The Stay will also be needed when exposing the dog to target animals later. Teach this Come-Sit-Stay exercise, (see pages 153-156) involving all family members, for at least a week before proceeding with the following part of the program.

Introducing "Prey" Animals

When you feel confident that your dog is orientated to you as leader, test it. Obtain the cooperation of the owner of another dog or cat (if they are your pet's prey) or get a chicken, hamster or other such animal and show your dog how to feel and behave around it. This is where the real essence of your relationship with your dog will become clear. You must be the dog's emotional leader, and you must act happy about the appearance of the other animal. However, before you undertake the introduction, make sure your set-up is secure for all concerned.

Safety First

Here are some ways to make the initial exposures to prey animals. These provide safety in the event the dog over-rides your control:

- Have your dog on leash, if suitable barriers are not available.
- Have the prey animal on leash or in an enclosure that cannot be broken through.
- With small breeds, have a sliding glass door between the animals. This may not suffice with larger dogs, if they charge the glass.
- Hold the target animal yourself.

Whatever your situation dictates, make the set-ups so that you can be in control.

The Jolly Routine

When your dog first notices the other animal, you must act happy about it. Get a ball or some other toy that your dog enjoys and bounce or toss it. Dominate the emotion of the occasion. Get your dog involved with *you*, rather than the other animal. The moment your dog pays attention to you, praise it and pet it briskly. When this is achieved, take away the other animal. Allow three hours to pass before beginning another Jolly Routine.

Follow this plan until the mere appearance of the prey animal turns your pet's attention to you, rather than toward it. At this point you can start bringing the two closer together. You may also benefit from standing alongside the other animal, facing your dog. This side-by-side approach causes your dog to see you with the other animal, showing friendliness. When your dog appears to accept the former prey, you should stop the session happily and remove the target animal or your dog, whichever situation fits your set-up.

Beware Attack Training

Be sure not to hold your dog on a tight leash as you approach the other animal. This is a classic method of training attack dogs. Many animal-killers will appear happy and delighted to be teased in this way. But, when given the freedom to get to the prey, they attack with heightened ferocity.

Habits to Correct

If you are in the habit of walking your dog in the neighborhood, this must be stopped, as well as allowing any urination off your own property. Most animal-killers have extended their rightful home boundaries by wetting their "brands" outside their own area.

If your dog "worries" a fence line by pacing, running, or barking, keep it inside as much as possible and supervise its time in the yard with play. Practice Come-Sit-Stay in the area and get its mind off the barrier.

This program will require a minimum of three and a maximum of six weeks' practice to succeed. Even then, periodic refresher sessions are helpful for permanent rehabilitation.

Old Age Problems

When does old age begin in a dog? It varies, by breed. Here are the most obvious signs:

- Graying of the coat
- Cataracts
- Loosening of teeth
- Physical stiffness
- Increased sleeping and less activity

With these as signposts, a student of dogs can quickly recognize that some breeds age more quickly than others, especially the larger breeds, such as St. Bernards and Great Danes. Little dogs not only live longer, but also show signs of old age later. So, size and health care probably influence longevity more than any other factors. Let's examine some of the problems that can accompany aging in dogs.

BLINDNESS

As with people, many dogs gradually lose their sight as they age. However, the dog has another sense that can take the place of a cane to sense things it might bump into when making its way about the house or yard—its keen sense of smell. In fact, you may have noticed that blind dogs usually keep their noses to the floor or ground as they walk about. This allows them to smell the familiar pathways and avoid objects.

I have found another scent-aid that makes life a little easier for blind dogs. This was successful with our Dalmatian, who went blind at six years of age, but led a fairly active life for another four and a half years. Here is the system.

Apply a scented polish to all upright obstacles in the house and outdoors. This includes chair legs, door jambs, TV sets, etc. The dog will quickly identify this scent with things that are "up-and-down" and avoid them.

For horizontal dangers, such as steps, wires and low walls, apply a different scent. I used to spray such things with a mildly scented hair spray about once a week. It did the trick nicely and saved a lot of nose scrapes.

Voice Contact

As dogs go blind they may appear to become easily startled, especially when touched unexpectedly. I have seen this lead to biting in some cases. So, the rule with blind dogs is always to speak to them before touching them. If this is practiced, you will soon see the dog moving its head to "feel" for the hand that is going to touch it. This is especially true with strangers. When introducing your blind dog to strangers, have them sit in a familiar place and speak to the dog. Have them hold their hand below the level of the dog's chin, palm up, so the dog can find it by scent and nuzzle it.

Some blind dogs seem bothered by having the tops of their heads or backs petted; confine the petting to under the chin, on the throat and chest. This keeps the blind dog's head up and seems to relieve any worries it might have.

Blind dogs may also need "company" when going out to their toilet places. If this is a problem, it is best to put the animal on a twice-a-day feeding schedule and develop a twice-a-day rhythm for bowel movements. Be sure not to overfeed the dog. Feed just the amount that produces a formed, firm stool. Above all, be sure to leash a blind dog in areas that could be dangerous.

DEAFNESS

Whether old or young, deaf dogs can be taught by capitalizing on their vision. Body language and hand signals can speak like thunder to these animals. However, avoid shouting at partially or totally deaf dogs. Shouting can confuse them, and they often respond by barking. And nothing is worse than a constantly barking deaf dog—everyone is bothered by it but the dog!

The deaf dog must learn to pay visual attention to you at all times when you are out with it. To teach this, get some dried beans and make several small beanbags. Then take the dog to a safe area and, each time the dog takes its eyes off you, toss a beanbag at its legs. When it responds, you must crouch down and make "come-hither" gestures with your hands. Do not lean or move toward the dog, as this tells it to back up away from you. Have at least one of these "pay attention to me" sessions daily, concluding each session when your pet keeps its attention on you for several minutes without the beanbags.

After a few of these lessons, you should notice your pet keeping its attention on you without your having to toss a single bag. You will then have succeeded.

Proceed to places with stronger distractions until you are sure of the dog's attention at all times, under all conditions. In dangerous areas, such as next to streets, it is a good idea to keep a leash, perhaps even up to thirty feet long, on the dog. This provides maximum safety. Once you have your deaf dog's attention, teaching it to Sit-on-sign is relatively simple.

INCONTINENCE

Lack of bladder or bowel control can occur in dogs of any age. Your veterinarian can advise you about special treatments, such as low doses of female hormones for females who cannot control their urine, geriatric vitamin supplements and special diets. Whether the problem is with urine or stools, the doctor's diet must be carefully followed.

Overfeeding in cases of bowel incontinence is a no-no. The amount fed must produce a stool that is firm. Your pet will have difficulty exercising any control over loose stools. Once the quantity and consistency of the diet are well established, elimination should begin to stabilize and become regular. When this point is reached, proper supervision is all that is needed for success.

Toilet Supervision

Toilet time and place should be as consistent as possible. If necessary, feed your pet in a spot handy (but not too close) to its toilet area. This proximity often has created a habit of evacuating immediately

after eating—a most desirable result, since you must be home to feed the pet, and it is little bother then to supervise the toilet activities.

Bladder incontinence can be more difficult to control. If veterinary advice allows it, water can be made available only at meal times and before bedtime. However, the doctor must approve and set the schedule. It is most helpful if the incontinent pet is taken to its toilet place at the following times:

- After waking (even from a nap)
- After eating or drinking
- Following any play or unusual excitement
- After any extensive chewing activity
- Before bedtime.

Happy, sincere praise must be given when the "duty" is concluded at the proper place. If you focus your initial praise at the very spot that has been soiled, the dog may come over and sniff it. That is good, since it helps to fix the spot in the animal's memory bank, via its keen sense of smell.

In some cases where physical control is literally impossible, the problem will persist. In these situations; inexpensive pet diapers, available from the doctor or pet store, can be used to contain the problem. Urine or a formed stool will not be cripplingly unpleasant for the animal.

IRRITABILITY

Many dogs grow old with full vigor and remain in excellent spirits. Others, for various reasons, become more retiring and seem to seek solitude or, at least, peace and quiet. Some of these may object to being disturbed. Keeping in mind that old age has its own set of behavioral rules, the best advice is to follow the old rule and let sleeping dogs lie. A little crotchetiness in old age is not news to anyone over the age of reason. If there are children in the house with such a pet, they should be taught to leave the animal alone. If this is impossible, such as may be the case with nonfamily children, the dog should then be separated from the area to avoid any harassment.

It bears repeating, especially in cases of elderly pets, that veterinary care often must be intensified for their well-being, their behavioral acceptability and our own peace of mind. It is an excellent practice to report to the doctor gross or even mild changes in the behavior or condition of your pet.

As in cases of incontinence, it takes just a little understanding and consideration to afford your pet the luxury of growing old with dignity and grace. In families with children, such a program instills respect for the elderly, one of civilized humankind's most laudable traits.

PART III

Correction Programs
for
Behavior Problems in Cats

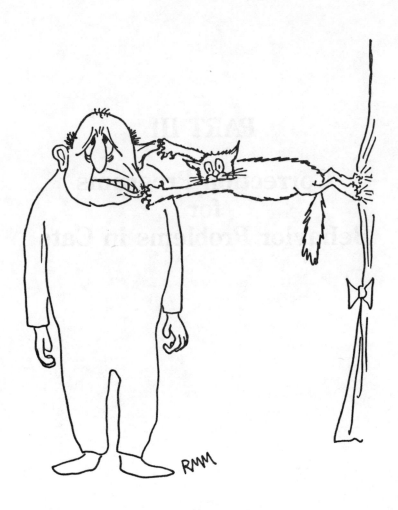

"He's been depressed ever since we got the T.V. The Tom and Jerry cartoons . . .
The cat never wins!"

Behavior Problems in Cats

INTRODUCTION

The following three programs for behavior problems in cats are children of necessity. Through my years of helping dog owners, I naturally found that many of these people also had problem cats. The four main difficulties mentioned always were: housetraining kittens, housesoiling by older cats, clawing and suckling, and aggression toward owners. Programs for correcting these are based on the same concepts used for dog problems, but without the "learn to earn praise and petting" element.

A common element in correcting cat problems is that of intensive daily play sessions. This only takes a few minutes—five at the most—but for some reason it is absolutely necessary for success. Don't skip it!

Another serious cat behavior problem is that of fighting other cats. I have but one humane correction, and it is 100% successful. Keep your cat indoors. If you have two pet cats who are fighting, you can try the Fighting program for dogs, substituting the play sessions for earning praise, but success with this has been limited.

"I've always hated cats . . . but this one is different . . . kind of like a dog."

Housetraining

When a cat starts urinating inside its home, it is trying to apply its personal "brand" on the territory. This is true whether the cat is male or female, neutered or not. It is a sort of feline "Mark of Zorro," saying in the most primitive way, "I am here and here to stay!"

The reasons for this problem range from under- to over-indulgence by people, or the presence of another cat's urine inside or outside the home. From the pet's point of view the behavior is natural, and gives temporary relief from feelings of insecurity about its territory. However, the staining and odor accompanying it provide cat owners with nothing but eyesores and offended nostrils.

PUDDLES

Simple puddles of urine around the home are different from spraying. If your problem is puddles, you will need to provide your pet with a simple housetraining plan centered on a litter box or a designated toilet area. It is not difficult. Most cats, given a chance to dig a little hole in the area, will soon acquire a lifelong habit of using it. The trick in establishing the habit is to praise the pet immediately after it has completed its duty—right there at that place—not when it has left the area.

Along with this procedure it is of utmost importance to keep the litter box or other area cleaned up daily. Further, the litter material must be replaced with clean material at least once a week, depending on the area's size and the size of your pet. Big cats soil litter more quickly than do tiny cats or kittens. So, as kittens mature, it may be necessary to change from once-a-week renewal to a twice-a-week schedule. In my experience this is the single most overlooked aspect of raising and training cats.

So many of my clients have said, "Tabby was just perfect for the first six months, and then this terrible soiling started around the house!" Often we forget that our kittens so soon become cats.

Cleanup

Another important step is proper cleanup of accidents, whether from puddling, defecation or spraying behavior. Although there are available several commercial liquids for cleaning, plain lukewarm water mixed half and half with white vinegar is about as effective as anything. This mixture should be doused or sponged generously on the area so as to dilute the offensive residue. Allow it to remain for about ten minutes, then completely blot it up with paper towels until dry to the touch. Then repeat the process.

During the cleanup the pet should be kept in an area where it cannot witness these activities concerning its urine or defecation. This is just in case your cat may find that your interest in the place stimulates an urge to refresh the spot.

SPRAYING

To solve the problem of spraying urine, you will need to consider the total life you are leading with your pet. The arrival of a new baby, another pet or houseguests may result in the cat's getting less attention than it is accustomed to receiving. If this is the case, make it a point to have a couple of play sessions each day. Use a favorite toy and really get involved with your pet for a few minutes in each session.

If you think you are doting too heavily, petting too much, or otherwise overindulging your cat, taper off gradually from the stroking and petting and introduce the play sessions. Play is a most necessary aspect of life to many cats. Too often as our kittens grow up, we forget about playing. Quite naturally, the cat feels the loss. The result can be spraying. Play sessions have proved most valuable in solving the problem.

FEEDING

Besides play sessions and applying proper cleanup procedures, another step should be taken, which involves feeding. Cats are basically fastidious about their toilet habits. They are loathe to eliminate in the same area as they eat. Given the opportunity to be hygienic, cats will be so. Therefore, the final step in solving the spraying behavior exploits this tendency.

If your pet has a favorite spot for its spraying, feed it at that spot, after properly cleaning the area. If it has two spots, split each feeding into two dishes and place them at the spots. Leave the dishes down between feedings, washing them before each feeding time.

"Tootsie-pie's going to be spaded, just like Mother!"

This should be done until four days have passed during which the cat has not soiled in these areas. Then resume feeding at the regular place.

If your pet regresses and soils or sprays again, restart the spot-feeding program until another four days' perfect performances have been achieved. Then, go back to feeding at the regular location. Keep this up until the problem is resolved.

In case you wondered, the most spray areas an owner had to deal with in this plan is 13. That is, the pet's food ration was split among 13 dishes! Though the problem had existed for two years, it took only two weeks for it to clear up. So it was worth applying the entire program.

SPAY OR NEUTER?

If your pet is not neutered, discuss this aspect with your veterinarian. In my experience, unless you are a cat breeder, neutering is the kindest step. It alleviates the frustrations of thwarted sexual drives, whether in male or female. Proper postoperative care and feeding as advised by your veterinarian will avoid obesity later on. Also, your pet will lead a much more contented life.

"I have the feeling that in this dispute over castrating the cat, neither of you is thinking particularly of the cat."

Clawing and Suckling

The annual national cost in furniture, drapes, clothing and other household items destroyed by the clawing or suckling of pet cats amounts to many millions of dollars. Fortunately, most cats are open and display the misbehavior in front of people. Correction is simple at these times.

CORRECTION METHODS

Most owners distract the cat by saying "No," picking it up, moving it and swatting it on the rear end. The clever cat owner distracts the animal with some sound or object that cannot be associated with themselves personally (which is more likely to be effective when the owner is away) and then introduces some object that the cat is urged to claw or suckle, such as a scratching post, toy or ball.

The secret of successful corrections is to use a distraction that is effective not only when you are there, but also when you are *not* there. With this in mind, it becomes obvious that it is wiser to toss a small pillow when the cat starts to misbehave than to shout its name and "No!" The "No" will be effective, but it is dependent on your presence to succeed. The pillow, if tossed without the animal seeing you handle it, will still be present to remind the cat even when you are away.

Relieving Tension

The principles for stopping a kitten or adult cat suckling or clawing are:

- Establish a satisfying daily playtime routine.
- Correct the behavior when you are home with an element that is still evident when you are away from home.

If these two steps are carried out, the cause (tension) as well as the habit will be treated.

Use of Play

Cats, kittens and people benefit from play. The happiness generated between your pet and you during playtimes satisfies a basic social feline and human need. The result is a more relaxed pet, one less likely to have built-up tensions caused by social isolation and other stresses of life with people.

The second step, correcting the overt behavior itself, becomes less necessary when the first principle is applied. However, some corrections may be necessary, so here is a plan that has succeeded in hundreds of cases where punishment systems had failed.

Along with the distractions via sounds or articles not associated with you, as mentioned earlier, a few substances have been helpful, when applied properly.

Many cats seem to hate the taste and odor of Listerine, and most cats dislike intensely the sensation of alum when they taste it. It tends to pucker the mouth's membranes, and is the main ingredient in underarm deodorants. Using either of these substances, follow this routine for four days and see if the clawing or suckling abates or disappears.

When the kitten or cat is not in the room to witness it, lightly spray Listerine or a super-dry deodorant on the articles that the animal has been working on. If Listerine is used, dilute it 50/50 with water and lightly spray it on the articles. If the materials could be stained, do not use it. Stay with the underarm deodorant instead. You may want to use an unscented variety to avoid having a room that smells like a perfume factory.

Test Your Success

For four days, hold daily play sessions (mornings are most effectively relaxing for this) and apply the spray, then stop the spraying and see if the corrections (playtimes and spraying) have achieved success.

If correction is total, suspend everything but the playtimes. If less than successful, apply the spray and playtime routine for another four days. Then test the degree of success once more.

After four days to six weeks, you should have the problem totally corrected. In the event of backsliding later, which can occur due to changes in the family routine, or the presence of guests or other animals around the house, simply reinstate the program and success should be realized shortly.

Opening Views

If your pet is clawing at drapes, curtains or shades because of some attraction outside a window, correction may be more difficult. If you cannot control the animals or people that attract it, and if the spray does not succeed, you may be best advised to move the curtains or drapes aside before you leave home. At least this will save your materials in addition to removing the visual barriers for the cat.

Remember Play

One of the easiest and therefore most common oversights in living with cats involves playtimes. The simple act of tossing a toy or ball achieves more than an emotional release for your cat. Exercise, so essential to good health, is generated. The reflexes in developing kittens are stimulated toward full scope. Inner tensions are relieved and emotional stability is therefore maintained. Most successful playtimes require only 5 to 15 minutes to attain their full benefits.

Throughout your program remain optimistic and good natured. Your mood affects your pet and brings results even more quickly.

"Be careful, Doctor, she doesn't like men!"

Aggression Toward Owners

To understand and deal with the problem of feline viciousness toward people, it is necessary first to appreciate the cat's emotional makeup regarding defensive and aggressive behavior. Then the course to follow becomes sensible.

DEFENSE—OFFENSE

Cats, quite rightly, defend their physical safety when threatened. Most of us have had the experience of trying to get a cat out from under furniture, down from a tree or out of a cage. To some pets this approach appears threatening, and they respond with typical feline hissing, growling, arched back and bared claws. Though it appears aggressive, it is in fact defensive behavior. It is defensive because, if we back away and remove our threat, the cat calms down.

On the other hand, if we make the same approach, receive the same hostile display, back away from the cat and then are pursued by the raging animal, we become the victim of aggressive behavior. And few things in life are more awe-inspiring than being attacked by an offensive cat.

As with most animals, including the human species, once a rage starts it is like an avalanche. It seems to have to run its course. In the interim, severe damage to the target of the fury usually occurs. Fortunately, there are few cases of such aggression by cats toward people. More common is the problem of aggression induced by affection.

A SAD CASE

Most cats, when sexually aroused, show aggressive tendencies. Here is an actual case that may parallel some of your own experiences.

Mrs. X was comfortably settled before her television set for the evening when Toby jumped onto her lap, which was his usual habit. As he lay there Mrs. X began stroking him absent-mindedly. Toby began to purr graciously, seeming to enjoy the affection in his normal way. After a few minutes Toby began kneading with his forepaws on Mrs. X's bathrobe.

She stopped stroking and said, "No, Toby. Be a good boy."

Toby responded by withdrawing his claws, whereupon Mrs. X turned her attention back to the TV and started stroking her pet again.

What Mrs. X did not appreciate was that Toby had started, then interrupted, a feline precopulatory aggressive display. Most of our cats handle these situations quite well. It is when they do not that trouble results, as on this occasion.

As Mrs. X continued softly petting Toby, he resumed his contented purring, but now began salivating as well. A few minutes more and Toby was applying his claws more vigorously, right through Mrs. X's rather thick bathrobe, scratching her skin. Her response was the same as had happened many times before.

She stopped stroking Toby and said, "Ouch! You hurt me. You're a bad boy and now you have to get down."

She grabbed the aroused pet to put him off her lap and was horrified to hear an outraged feline scream, after which he fastened both claws and fangs deep into her forearm!

She tried to shake him off in vain, grabbed him by the scruff of the neck with her other hand and then started screaming herself. She tugged even harder with her free hand and literally tore the enraged cat from her arm, whereupon he turned and dug in again, but this time on Mrs. X's face!

Now Mrs. X's screams were even louder than the cat's as she felt fangs sinking into the flesh of her right eyebrow and eyelid. With both hands, summoning all her strength, she again ripped the cat from her flesh and threw the snarling animal across the room.

When he hit the floor Toby reeled, snarled and started racing back toward his owner.

Mrs. X ran for her apartment's front door. As her bloodsmeared hand turned the knob she felt Toby attacking her calf. She struggled through the door, closed it on her leg and, using the door jamb as leverage, scraped the snarling cat from her calf and ankle. The door closed and Mrs. X sank to the floor in hysterical tears.

Fortunately, her neighbors insisted she go with them to the emergency hospital immediately. Otherwise Mrs. X might have reentered her apartment too early to avoid another attack, because Toby was heard yowling for a full 15 minutes before he quieted. When she did enter the apartment, it was with the aid of her landlord, who carried a large, thick blanket, ready to wrap up Toby in the event he was still aggressive. Much to their amazement, Toby was lying on the couch, serenely grooming himself. He was his old self again.

At this point Mrs. X telephoned her veterinarian and was referred to me.

Sexual Basis

I mention this gory story to illustrate the primitive nature of our feline friends regarding sexual stimulation. We have all witnessed or at least heard the extremely aggressive outbursts between mating cats. This behavior is controlled by hormones. Petting often triggers internal hormone responses in cats that, in turn, lead to aggressive behavior. Unfortunately, once the surge of these hormones begins, it appears to have to run its course in some animals. Mrs. X's Toby just happened to be in a state of ripe hormonal readiness for its unfortunate avalanche of rage.

Once his behavior was understood, Mrs. X asked the predictable question: "Do I have to give up petting Toby or be attacked every time by him?"

The answer, of course, is "No," but with qualifications. Here is the plan that has been highly successful in severe cases such as Mrs. X's, as well as less dramatic situations.

One common element in most aggressive cats is a lack of proper play between the owner and the pet. A short (5-15 minutes) play session revolving around a toy or ball of yarn must be started immediately. This helps the cat exercise and express playful aggression toward something other than its owner.

Neutering Can Help

In the case of intact male cats, I recommend neutering as an aid. Sexually stimulated aggression can be lowered substantially, sometimes totally, through neutering. Unless the male is valuable breeding stock, it is the kindest step to take, since an intact tom suffers when it cannot fulfill its sexual aims. Cat fights and urination around the house when a female cat is nearby are two of the most common side effects of this frustration. Your veterinarian can advise you of other benefits and help in dietary planning to avoid the obesity many owners fear is inevitable after neutering.

Control Petting

Besides the daily play sessions and neutering, the third step of this plan involves controlling your own method of petting your cat. Most of us are extremely sensitive to the moods of our pets. Therefore, when you feel that the cat is in one of "those" moods, make the petting brisk and quick—no more than five to ten seconds. At other times, longer stroking is all right, except when the cat starts that tell-tale kneading behavior with its forepaws, starts salivating, or seems otherwise to be getting aroused. The activity must then be shifted from stroking to play with one of the favorite aggression-objects we discussed earlier.

When this plan is followed faithfully, the result can be a cat that is affectionate, fun to be with and no longer a threat to your well-being.

Helpful Reading

Campbell, W.E.: *Behavior Problems in Dogs*. American Veterinary Publications, Santa Barbara, 1975.

Mery, F.: *The Life, History and Magic of the Dog*. Grossett & Dunlop, New York, 1970.

Scott, J.P. and Fuller, J.P.: *Dog Behavior: The Genetic Basis*. University of Chicago Press, Chicago, 1965.

Shah, I.: *The Sufis*. Doubleday, New York, 1962.

Tuttle, J.L., editor: *Dogs Need Our Love*. Libra, Roslyn Heights, NY, 1983.

About the Author

Bill Campbell's early background was in TV and radio writing and broadcasting. Later, after training in industrial psychology, he conducted human motivation programs for seven years.

Bill worked for four years at the Canine Behavior Institute in Los Angeles with its founder, Dare Miller, Ph.D. He later established the Dog Owner Guidance Service at Sun Valley Ranch. He became a contributing editor of *Modern Veterinary Practice* magazine, and in 1975 published *Behavior Problems in Dogs*. That same year he helped found the American Society of Veterinary Ethology.

Bill and his wife Peggy now live on a wooded ranch near Grants Pass, Oregon. Bill lectures, consults and writes for *Modern Veterinary Practice, DogWorld* magazine, and other publications. He and Peggy market the *BehavioR$_x$* series of dog and cat behavior brochures, which are available from many veterinary hospitals.

About the Illustrator

Dr. Bob Miller (RMM) cartooned his way through the Colorado State University School of Veterinary Medicine, graduating in 1956. He has practiced in Thousand Oaks, California, ever since, where his daily practice experiences serve as inspiration for his cartoons and writing. American Veterinary Publications (Santa Barbara, CA) has published five books of his cartoons and comic verse. His cartoons have appeared regularly in *Modern Veterinary Practice* and other magazines, and he writes a monthly column for *Veterinary Medicine*. In 1985 his autobiographical book, *Most of My Patients are Animals* (Paul S. Ericksson, Middlebury, VT) was published, with an introduction by his friend and colleague, James Herriot.

INDEX

DOGS

A

adopting an older dog, 123-126
aggression, 45-48, 58, 65, 75, 77, 88, 90, 229-234, 247-250, 251-254
allelomimetic behavior, 59-60

B

babies and dogs, 195-198
balance, sense of, 35
barking, 14-24, 68, 163-176
begging, food, 148
behavior consultant, selection, 100-107
biting, 32, 42-43, 80, 177-181, 229-234
blindness, 259-260
body language, canine, 72-85
body language, human, 86-90, 189
bossiness, see dominance

C

cars
    chasing, 191-193
    riding in, 119, 124, 167

carsickness, 119, 199-202
chasing
    bicycles, 48
    cars, 48, 191-193
    people, 48, 56
chewing objects, 53-54, 94, 101, 169-172
chewing self, 221-224
children, 104, 106, 198
"Come," 93, 131-132, 153
consistency, owner, 104
coprophagia, 209-216
courtship behavior, 32

D

deafness, 260-261
defense reflexes, 40-42
defensiveness, 66, 79, 89
digging, 101, 185, 213-216
direction, sense of, 34
dog-door, 144, 185, 213
dominance, canine, 54, 56, 69-70, 75, 78, 81, 83
door, dashing out, 236-237
dreaming, 63

Want to know more about your Dog?

The following titles may be ordered direct, or purchased at your local bookstore or pet supply shop:

YES! Please send me:

Qty.

____ **How to Raise A Puppy You Can Live With.** Rutherford & Neil. $7.98

____ **All-Breed Dictionary of Unusual Names.** Gloria Jarrett. $9.98

____ **Your Dog & The Law.** Murray Loring, J.D., D.V.M. $9.98

____ **Canine Hip Dysplasia and Other Orthopedic Diseases.** Lanting. $14.98

____ **Canine Reproduction: A Breeder's Guide.** Phyllis Holst, M.S., D.V.M. $17.98

____ **Positively Obedient: Good Manners for the Family Dog.** Barbara Handler. $8.98

Please add $2.00 per order under $20.00; $3.00 per order over $20.00. Colorado residents please add 3% sales tax.

☐ Payment enclosed☐ Please charge my: ☐ Visa ☐ MasterCard

Acct #_____ Exp. Date_____

Signature _____

Name _____

Address _____

City _____ State _____ Zip _____

Mail to:

Alpine Publications, Inc., 2456 E. 9th St., Loveland, CO 80537